大夏书系·英语教学

玩游戏，学英语

英语课堂游戏活动100例

王瑛 主编

华东师范大学出版社
全国百佳图书出版单位
·上海·

本书编委

主　　编　王　瑛

编　　委（按姓氏笔画排序）

郑雪莹　倪　静　唐晓艳

黄思佳　龚夏欢

目　录　CONTENTS

Part Two Vocabulary（词汇）

Part Three Grammar（语法）

Part Four Reading and Writing（读写）

Part Five Language Function（语言功能）

Introduction（序）
用英语游戏为教与学赋能

历时一年的酝酿及撰写，《玩游戏，学英语：英语课堂游戏活动 100 例》一书终于定稿了，回顾从选题、定题、写稿、改稿的经历与感受，我们有激动、有兴奋、有抓狂、有想放弃，然而更多的是有收获与成长。本册书编写团队是 1+5 模式，一位教研员加五位一线优秀青年教师，他们是上海市平和双语学校的黄思佳、上海市建平实验中学的唐晓艳、上海市张江集团中学的龚夏欢、上海市傅雷中学的郑雪莹、上海市万祥学校的倪静。这一次担任主编的经历，让我感受到了一些“纠结”与“惊喜”。在此，选其中一二与读者分享。

“纠结”之一——如何定题？如何定板块？

本书的关键词是游戏。游戏在辞海中的定义是：以直接获得快感为主要目的，且必须有主体参与互动的活动。德国生物学家谷鲁斯认为，游戏不是没有目的的活动，游戏并非与实际生活没有关联。如果把游戏活动纳入课堂教学，那就是教学的一部分，也需要考虑游戏的目的和真正作用。在为本书定书名时我们经历了头脑风暴，想出了很多备选，如：《玩转课堂》《知“英”识趣》《“娱”教“娱”乐》《英语还可以这样学——好用的英语游戏活动集锦》《英语小游戏》《玩转大课》《“趣”学英语——英语游戏活动荟萃》《课堂游戏这样玩才有戏》《实用英语课堂游戏 100 例》《玩游戏，学英语》《玩转英语课堂之 100 个趣味游戏》《趣味英语课堂游戏集锦》《游戏课堂——让学生爱上英语多一个理由》，等等。最终确定了目前读者所看到的此书名。

如何定板块？也是让人很纠结。是按照游戏类别分？还是按照课前、课中、课后分？在听取一线老师的需求和编写团队多次研讨后，我们最终确定按照语音、词汇、语法、读写、语言功能五个板块进行划分。这样做的目的是为了方便教师检索和阅读，也使教师更明晰游戏活动指向什么语言知识及语言技能等。

“纠结”之二——写哪些内容？体例如何定？

在写作前，我们也进行过调研，发现写游戏类的文章及书籍有很多专家和老师已涉及，所以，要写出自己的特色并不是件容易的事。首先是内容。大版块确定后，选定具体的游戏内容是难点也是关键点。最后我们确定要写的内容须基于《义务教育英语课程标准》及教师的教学需求，能切实为中小学英语教师设计学习活动提供参考，使这些活动能运用于教学实际，同时也可以为教师打开教学思路，提升他们的教学设计能力。另外，在设计中我们也希望能体现跨学科意识及中国传统文化的传承。

所有的游戏我们都用简明、地道的英语撰写，并附有中文旁注和说明。游戏活动包含游戏名称、游戏目标、活动水平、活动时长、活动步骤等。书中还提供了一些游戏所需的学习单、任务单及教学示例等，这些资源可以帮助教师在实际教学中明确如何实施，帮助教师更好地开展游戏活动。

在纠结之余，作为主编的我也有惊喜。最初华东师范大学出版社的编辑任红瑚老师向我约稿时，我还有疑虑，有必要去写游戏活动吗？总觉得近几年教师关注得更多的热点是针对各个课型的研究。之后又担心能写出100个游戏活动吗？但在整个编写、审读过程中我常常感叹“原来可以这样教！”“原来可以这样做啊！”基层老师的确是宝藏，后浪的力量也让人备感欣慰。

此书能够顺利付梓，要感谢的人很多。首先感谢编写团队的青年教师们，利用工作之余，贡献出自己的智慧；也感谢责任编辑任红瑚的鼓励及精益求精的专业精神。

鉴于团队编写成员的水平有限，书中难免存在错误、缺漏等问题，敬请各位读者提出宝贵意见。

王　瑛

2021 年 12 月

Part One

Phonetics
（语音）

1 Don't Catch Me!

Focus: Learning Phonetic Symbols

Level: Lower-intermediate

Duration: 10～15 minutes

Procedure:

- Four volunteers stand on the stage and each is given a card with a phonetic symbol on it.
- The teacher walks towards one of the four students and tries to catch him/her. In order not to be caught, the student must speak out one of the phonetic symbols on his/her opponent's card. If the student read the phonetic symbol correctly, the teacher will turn around and catch his/her opponent.
- The student who stays on the stage till the end is the winner.

○ 在游戏之前，教师可以在全班范围内先教授游戏中所需要用到的音标。

Examples:

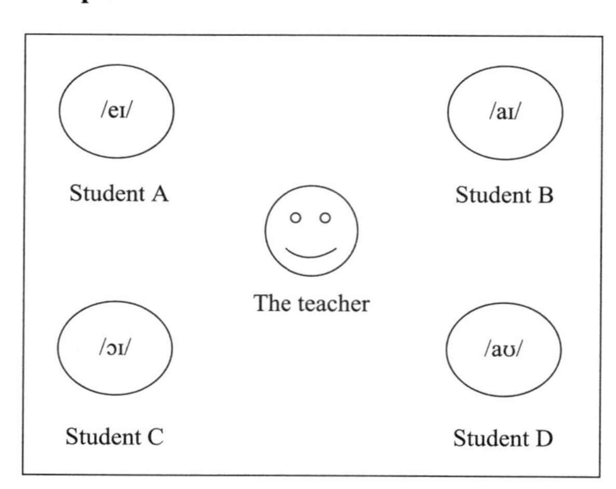

○ 图中是以四个音标为示例，教师也可以根据自己的教学目标和重点，增加和减少音标数量。如果是一阶段的音标复习课，可以增加音标数量，扩大参与度。

这个游戏叫做“别抓我”，学生要在这个游戏中不被抓到，就必须读出对手所持有的音标。通过这样的方式，促进学生努力去学习和记忆音标。

这个游戏规则比较简单，但是可玩性比较强，非常适合运用于低年级学生对于音标的学习。对于低年级的学生来说，单一的模仿、朗读，可能会比较枯燥乏味，但是通过这种在课堂中动起来的方式，可以激发他们内心的挑战欲，促进他们主动学习。当然，在热闹的游戏之后，教师也需要再用领读、跟读等方式，复习本堂课的教学内容。

2 Do You Remember Me?

Focus: The Revision of Phonetic Symbols

Level: Lower-intermediate

Duration: 10～15 minutes

Procedure:

- Nine cards with different phonetic symbols are posted face down on the blackboard in advance.
- The teacher reads a phonetic symbol and students in different groups take turns to turn over the cards on the blackboard.
- If the correct phonetic symbol is found, the student can win one point for his/her group. If not, the card should be put back until someone finds the correct one.
- The group with the highest points is declared as the winner.

○ 当学生所翻出的卡片内容并不是教师所读的音标时，这个卡片要被重新翻转到初始状态（即看不到音标的状态），这在一定程度上，促使所有同学努力地去记忆这些已经被翻出的音标卡片，而不仅仅是做一个旁观者。

Examples:

[æ]	[eɪ]	[ʌ]
[aɪ]	[e]	[ə]
[eɪ]	[æ]	[aɪ]

○ 教师可以通过选取不同的音标来把控这个游戏的难度。可以是九个不同的、容易混淆的音标；也可以减少数量，降低难度。

这个游戏叫做“你还记得我吗？”，这是一个记忆类的游戏，可以帮助学生复习所学过的音标。教师可以选取一定数量的音标，比如例子中的这几个比较容易混淆的元音来进行游戏，也可以通过减少音标的数量和易混淆程度来降低难度，逐步让学生适应。在课堂中，这个游戏可以全班学生参加，每个小组每次派一名代表，大家轮流来翻卡片，直到找到教师所读的音标卡片为止。

这个游戏的好处在于，学生不仅要仔细听清教师所读的音标，同时也要仔细观察其他同学所翻出的音标，并且努力记忆，避免自己再次翻到同样的卡片，从而增加胜算。通过这样的方式，虽然每次只是一位同学上前来翻卡片，但实际上所有的同学都参与其中。每当学生翻出一张卡片后，教师可以引导学生读出卡片上的音标并让学生判断是否找到了目标卡片。在一次次的翻转过程中，学生也在潜移默化地复习这些音标，达到巩固的目的。

这个游戏也可以在小组内完成，比如每四人一组，以桌游的形式来进行。一位学生可以扮演教师的角色，负责读音标，其他三位同学轮流翻转卡片。教师在这个过程中，只需巡视课堂，及时给予帮助即可。还可以在班级进行擂台赛，先在小组内决出胜负，再在班级内进行决赛，以提升学生的积极性和参与度。

3 Who's the Fastest?

Focus: The Revision of Phonetic Symbols

Level: Lower-intermediate

Duration: 10～15 minutes

Procedure:

- Write several phonetic symbols on the blackboard in a random fashion.
- Two volunteers come to the blackboard and each is given a flyswatter.
- The teacher reads the phonetic symbols randomly and the student hits the phonetic symbol with his/her flyswatter as quickly as possible. The student who first hits the correct phonetic symbol wins the game.
- The teacher can make the game more challenging by not reading the phonetic symbols directly

○ 这个游戏中的苍蝇拍只是一个道具，也可以用其他比较吸引学生的道具，比如充气榔头等。还可以要求学生用手拍黑板，只需学生反应迅速即可。

○ 教师可以通过改变指令的方式来控制这个游戏的难度。这个游戏的基础玩法是由教师直接读出音标；而进阶玩法则是由教师给出线索，让学生“抽丝剥茧”，确定音标。

but just giving hints for a particular phonetic symbol. When giving hints, the teacher can start with general ones and gradually get more specific. For example, the first hint can be "it is a vowel" and then followed by two examples such as "take" and "wake" . Thus, students can figure out the target phonetic symbol is "/eɪ/" .

Examples:

/eɪ/　　/aɪ/　　/aʊ/

/ɪə/　　/ɔɪ/　　/eə/

○ 示例中所选取的音标，是比较容易混淆的双元音，有一定挑战性。教师可以通过选取不同的音标，来控制游戏的难度。

这个游戏的名字为"谁最快"，这是一个考验学生反应力的游戏，以此来复习和巩固所学过的音标。游戏很简单，即比拼哪位同学可以最快反应出教师所说的音标。对于低年级或者是刚接触音标的学生来说，教师可以直接读出音标，以检测学生是否掌握。这个游戏也适用于较高年级的学生，教师只需改变指令，由直接读出音标，变为给出线索，让学生通过已知线索，一步步确定音标。通过这样的方式，可以增加游戏的挑战性和趣味性，吸引较高年级的同学参与。

另外，这个游戏的形式具有多样性。比如以学生个人为单位的挑战赛、擂台赛，最后决出班级冠军；也可以是以小组为单位，每两人一组，通过计分制来决出获胜小组。

4 Snakes and Ladders

Focus: The Revision of Phonetic Symbols

Level: Intermediate

Duration: 10~15 minutes

Procedure:

- All the students are divided into several groups and every two groups compete with each other based on a random draw. A student should be selected to play for his/her group. The rest of the group members

○ 这个游戏可以以小组对战的形式进行，也可以以双人对战的形式进行。

can be present at the match and offer help if necessary.

- Both players put their counters in the "Start" square. They take turns to roll the dice and move the counter to the target square according to the number of the dice.
- Each player must read the word as they arrive at the square. During this process, the group members have the rights to help the player. If the player makes it, he/she can go forward one square as a reward. Otherwise, he/she must take a step back.

○ 在读单词或者音标的过程中，场上玩家有向自己组内成员求助的机会，从而提升其他同学对于游戏的参与度。

- If a player lands on a snake's head, he/she has to "slide down" to the square containing the snake's tail. If a player lands on the bottom of a ladder, he/she can "climb" to the square containing the top of the ladder.

○ 蛇与梯的设置，增加了游戏的趣味性与不确定性。碰到蛇头，要滑落后退至蛇尾；而碰到梯子，则可以顺势向上。

- The first player to reach the "Finish" square is the winner.
- After the game, the teacher had better guide the students to summarize the phonetic symbols or pronunciations of different letters or combinations of letters in the words they came across in the game.

Examples:

16 cloud	17 house	18 bound	Finish
15 flour	14 couch	13 loud	12 mouth
8 count	9 pout	10 round	11 sound
7 shout	6 found	5 about	4 round
Start	1 proud	2 aloud	3 doubt

○ 示例所选取的单词中，都包含 ou 这个字母组合，且发音都为 /aʊ/。教师也可以自行选取其他单词，以呼应不同的教学目标和重点。

这个游戏的名字为“蛇与梯”，是一个经典的桌面游戏，以此为框架，将其与音标或单词结合，可以达到复习所学音标或读音规则的目的。

游戏可以以小组对战或者双人对战的形式进行。与大部分棋类游戏一样，这个游戏的目标是率先走到终点。参与者想要顺利向前走，则必须将对应格子中的单词或音标读准确。如果是以小组对战的形式进行，在读单词的过程中，小组成员可以帮助场上参与者读单词，以增加该游戏的参与度。而游戏中的蛇与梯，则为这个游戏增添了许多不确定性和趣味性。

教师可以根据自己的教学目标和教学重难点来设计格子内的单词或音标。针对低年级或者初学者，教师可以在格子内放入不同的音标，只要学生读对即可。而针对高年级学生，教师可以侧重于读音规则，比如可以放入带有同一个字母或者字母组合，但是却有着不同发音的单词。在示例单词中，所有字母组合 ou 的发音都是 /aʊ/，教师也可以加入其他带有字母组合 ou, 但是发音不相同的单词，如 cough, couple 等。在最后的总结环节，教师可以引导学生总结规律，巩固所学。

5 Odd One Out

Focus: Phonemic Awareness
Level: Intermediate
Duration: 10～15 minutes
Procedure:

- 6 volunteers come to the stage and each is given a card with a phonetic symbol. Five of the phonetic symbols are the same while only one of them is different. Only the volunteer knows what the phonetic symbol on his/her card is.

○ 这个游戏中，有两个层面的信息差：其一是台上同学只知道自己拿到的音标，不知他人的；其二是台下同学不知道台上同学所拿到的音标。

- Each volunteer takes turns to give an example of the phonetic symbol he/she has. After a round, the audience should tell who is the odd one out. That means they should make their choice about whose phonetic symbol is the different one.

- In order to stay on the stage as long as possible, the volunteers should listen to others carefully and try to cover all the phonetic symbols they hear. Meanwhile, the audience should also pay attention to what they hear and take some notes if necessary. In this way, they can wisely make judgments.

○ 由于信息的缺失，台上的同学要认真听其他同学的例子，以确保自己的例子中也包含了与其他同学一样的音标，尽量让自己不显得“格格不入”。

- If the one who has the different phonetic symbol remains on the stage till the end, he/she wins the game. If not, the students successfully finding the “faker” win the game.

Examples:

/s/	/s/	/s/
/s/	/s/	/z/

○ 在这个游戏中，教师所给出的两个音标，应该是可以在一个单词中同时出现的，否则就不具有可玩性。比如示例中，拿到 /z/ 这个音标的同学，就可以用 seize 来举例，以迷惑其他同学。

这个游戏名叫“找不同”，类似于近些年来非常流行的叫做“谁是卧底”的游戏，通过台上台下同学的互动和思考，合力找出那个格格不入的“卧底”，旨在训练学生辨别单词中所包含的音素，提升学生的音素意识。

与原版的“谁是卧底”游戏不同的是，在这个游戏中，观众不是知道答案的旁观者，而是和台上选手一样，也需要通过仔细去听那些单词所包含的音素，来逐步确定谁才是“卧底”。

要玩好这个游戏，参赛者与观众都要非常注意所听到的单词中包含的音素。作为参赛者，需要尽可能地仔细听别人所举例的单词，以逐步确定其他人所拿到的音标，确认自己是否为“卧底”，如果是，就要尽量在自己所说的单词中，包含其他参赛者的音标，以免被投票出局；而作为观众，则可以记录每一位参赛者所说单词中的音素，通过比对，迅速找出那个不一样的音标。可能在第一轮的时候，所有同学都会毫无头绪，但是随着游戏的进行，不断地排除，缩小范围，就会离答案越来越近。

这个游戏吸引人的部分，就是游戏中的信息差，可以促使参赛者和观众都仔细倾听，逐步推理；另外，对于“谁是卧底”这个答案的追寻，也会促使参赛者和观众之间的博弈，增加了游戏的趣味性和参与度。

6 Fruit Picking

Focus: Phonemic Awareness

Level: Intermediate

Duration: 10～15 minutes

Procedure:

- Divide the whole class into several groups.
- Post four pictures with fruit trees on the blackboard, including apple tree, orange tree, banana tree, and strawberry tree. Each fruit tree has a particular phonetic symbol and a specific number.
- Provide each group with a dice, including Arabic numerals (1, 2, 3, 4) on four facets and two facets with "Lucky" .
- A student rolls the dice and find the fruit tree according to the number shown on the dice. Then the student should speak out a word whose pronunciation includes the phonetic symbol shown on the fruit tree. If the student can correctly speak out one word, he/she can pick up one fruit from the fruit tree for his/her group.
- If the dice meets "Lucky" , the student can directly pick up one from any fruit trees.
- The group which picks up the most fruits can win the game.

○ 对于掷到"Lucky"的规则设置，教师也可以相应提高难度。比如，如果掷到"Lucky"，学生可以任选一个音标来举例，举例正确才可以得分。

Examples:

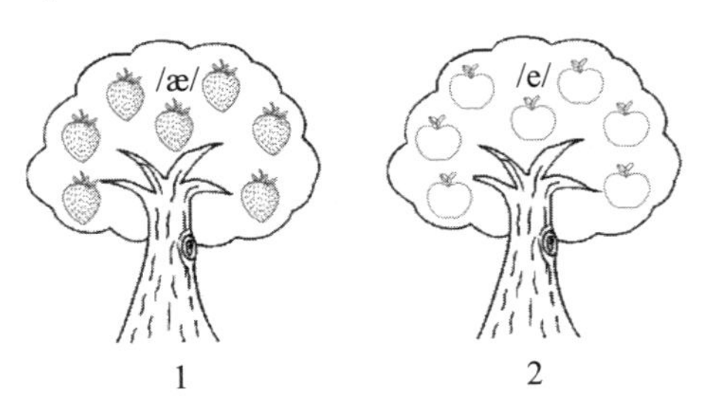

○ 教师可以准备一些立体的水果模型，以增加真实感；在教具有限的情况下，也可以让不同小组选择代表自己小组的颜色，用这个颜色来填涂水果，表示已经摘到这个水果。

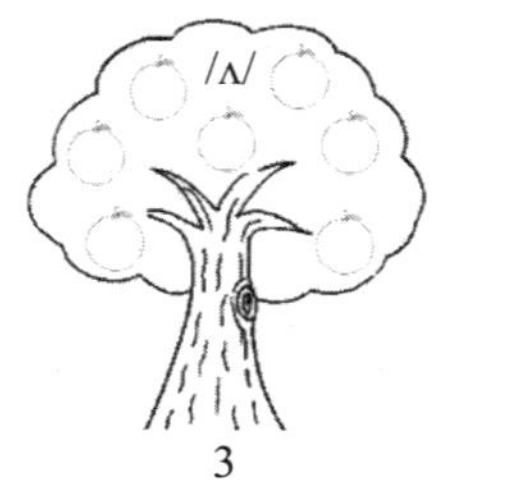

3

4

这个游戏叫做“摘水果”，游戏旨在通过竞赛的形式，鼓励学生说出含有目标音标的单词，提升学生的音素意识。

游戏可以以小组为单位进行，也可以以个人为单位进行。在新授音标时，这个游戏能够更好地帮助学生巩固所学，因为在听对手举例时，学生需要判断这个例子是否正确，这也是一种学习和复习的途径。

7 The Wolf Is Coming

Focus: Clarification of Some Similar Pronunciation
Level: Lower-intermediate
Duration: 10～15 minutes
Procedure:

- Select eleven volunteers. One acts as the wolf and the rest of them are divided into two groups. Group A is assigned to the phonetic symbol “/θ/” and group B is assigned to the phonetic symbol “/ð/” .

○ 教师可以根据自己的教学目标，选取不同的音标。

- The two groups stand in two parallel lines. Students from both groups take turns to compete in the game.
- The “wolf” randomly speaks out a word with the phonetic symbol “/θ/” or “/ð/” . If the pronunciation includes “/θ/” , the student from group A should run away at once in order not to be caught by the “wolf” and the student from group B should keep still.
- If the student from group A is caught by the “wolf” or the student from group

B makes the wrong action, he/she will be out.

- After five rounds, the group with more competitors on the stage wins the game.

Examples:

The words include the phonetic symbol "/θ/" :

thief	thank	think	thing	through
thin	mouth	throw	thirsty	breath

The words include the phonetic symbol "/ð/" :

they	those	brother	whether	other
that	breathe	another	these	further

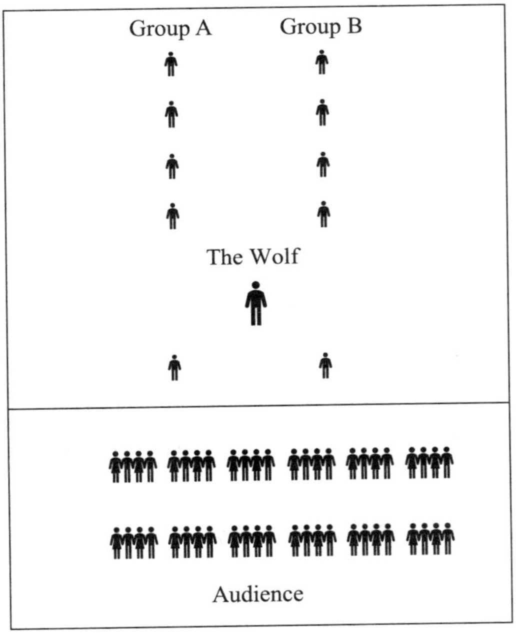

Group A　Group B

The Wolf

Audience

○ 教师可以根据教室的不同格局，变换游戏中学生的站位。但是扮演狼的学生需要与参与比拼的学生保持一米左右的距离，不宜过近或者过远。

这个游戏叫做"狼来了"，旨在让学生通过听音、辨音，区分一些比较容易混淆的音标。语音学习主要是通过模仿、朗读、背记等方式识读元音及辅音因素，通过对比、辨音、示例列举等方式归纳常见字母及字母组合的读音规则。在这个游戏中，为了不被"狼"抓到，学生需要仔细辨别"狼"所读的单词发音，以便做出正确的判断。比起传统的跟读、背记等方式，这个游戏大大地提升了学生学习的兴趣和参与度。

在几轮游戏过后，教师可以把所涉及的单词呈现在黑板或者屏幕上，带领学生进一步复习。

8 Better or Bitter?

Focus: Clarification of Some Similar Pronunciation
Level: Intermediate
Duration: 10～15 minutes
Procedure:

- Divide the whole class into several groups. Each student in the group takes turns to compete in the game.
- The teacher prepared ten sentences in advance. Each sentence is correct in grammar but contains an improper word whose pronunciation is similar to the correct word. For example, "The juice tastes much bitter so that all the children like it". In this sentence, the correct word should be "better". The mistake results from the confusion of the phonetic symbols "/e/" and "/ɪ/".
- The competitors should listen to the sentence carefully and notice the mistake as quickly as possible. The first one to point out the mistake and figure out the two confusing phonetic symbols can win a point for his/her group.
- The group with the highest points is the winner.

Examples:

(1) The juice tastes much bitter so that all the children like it. (bitter—better)

(2) I brought a lot of snakes to share with my classmates in the spring outing. (snakes—snacks)

○ 选取的例子尽量具有巨大的反差，这样更具戏剧效果，更易可以引起学生的兴趣。

(3) We listened to the school choir in the hole yesterday. What a wonderful performance! (hole—hall)

这个游戏译成中文，可以用"差之毫厘，谬以千里"来表示。游戏主要通过让学生仔细听老师朗读句子，找到其中的错误发音并纠正，达到帮助学生区分易混淆的音标的目的。

我们都知道，英语中的发音至关重要，如果我们在发音时不注意嘴型、发音位置、音的长短，就会导致很大的误差。这个游戏的有趣之处在于，用一些反差强烈的句子让学生去思考和体会，更能引发学生的兴趣。

这个游戏也可以倒过来玩，即让学生读句子，老师来改错或者小组之间互相来改错，增加互动性。如果时间充裕，还可以引导学生制作海报，将“一音之差”的两句话用简笔画的形式表现出来，也会具有较强的视觉冲击力。通过这些方式，学生会更加明晰发音的重要性。

9 Form a Word

Focus: Phonemic Awareness

Level: Intermediate

Duration: 10～15 minutes

Procedure:

- Twenty students stand in a circle with various stickers on them. Each sticker has a certain vowel or consonant on it.

○ 在游戏正式开始之前，教师可以引导学生先观察周围同学身上的音标，为接下来的活动作好准备。

- The teacher gives orders like “Two students form a word” . After hearing the order, the students should observe the stickers on other students and find the right phonetic symbol to form a correct word in thirty seconds. For example, the student whose sticker writes “/l/” should aim to find a certain vowel like “/ eɪ/ ” to form the word “lay” .
- After thirty seconds, the student who has found their partner should read and spell the word they form correctly, or they will be out. Undoubtedly, the student who is single will also be out.

○ 当已经组成组合的学生说出并拼读单词的时候，教师可以引导其他同学判断正误，增加参与度。

- The rest of the students take part in the next round. The teacher can change the order like “Three students form a word” to make the game more challenging.

Examples:

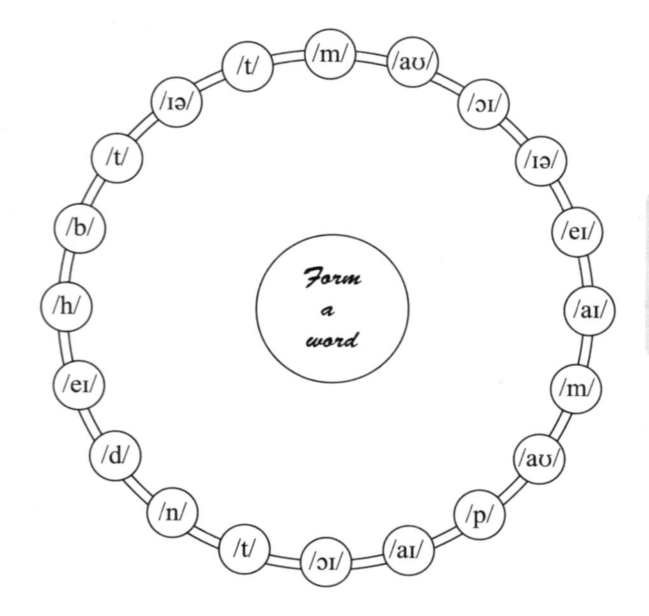

○ 教师应仔细斟酌所给出的音标卡片。比如图示中，有5个元音（出现两次）以及不甚相同的辅音，由此可以组成尽可能多的单词，保证学生可以至少玩两轮。

这个游戏的名字为“组单词”，旨在让学生通过观察、思考，将所学过的基本读音规则运用到实际中。《上海市初中英语学科教学基本要求》一书中指出：语音学习应该结合词汇、句子和语篇的学习来进行，要根据基本读音规则和国际音标认读单词，建立音与形的关系。学生如果想要在这个游戏中坚持到最后，就需要精准而快速地找到自己所需要的音标。而要做到这一点，首先要对基本读音规则有一定的掌握，并提前锁定自己所要找的目标音标。

教师在游戏之前，可以适当地提醒学生一些规律，比如常见的辅音 + 元音的组合。也就是说，如果一个学生代表的是一个辅音，那么他需要去找代表元音的同学来组成单词，这也是该游戏中比较重要的一个策略。

此外，学生在形成组合后，仍需要正确拼读出单词，才可以进入到下一轮。在拼读的过程中，参与游戏的同学可以再次体会音与形的关系，而在一旁观看的同学，也需要评判他们的拼读是否正确，由此，提升了整个游戏的参与度，其他同学也得到了练习的机会。

10 Feed the Cat

Focus: The Different Pronunciations of a Letter or Combination of Letters

Level: Low-intermediate

Duration: 10～15 minutes

Procedure:

- Divide the whole class into several groups. Each group is given several pens with a certain color.

○ 每一小组会得到不同颜色的笔，便于后续计分。

- Prepare several posters with a "cat" on them and post them on the wall. Each "cat" stands for a particular letter or combination of letters. Each letter or combination of letters has at least two different pronunciations. Students have to feed the "cat" with as much "fish" as possible. That means they ought to consider more examples of the varied pronunciations.
- After a group discussion, the students in each group should rush to the posters and write down the words which contain the letter or combination of letters.
- The more "fish" of different types students feed, the more pleased the "cat" will be. In order to satisfy the "cat" and get more points, students should think of more pronunciations of each letter or combination of letters. For example, if the "cat" stands for "ch", the student who writes down "/tʃ/" and "chair" can get two points for his or her group. The following students who write down "chat" can only get one point. But they can also think of another example such as "/ʃ/" and "machine" to get two points.

○ 在这个游戏中，如果一个小组率先举出了同一字母或者字母组合的不同发音的例子并正确写出了音标，这个小组得到的分数将翻倍，以此鼓励学生关注同一字母或者字母组合的不同发音。

- The group which contributes the most examples and gains the highest points can win the game.

Examples:

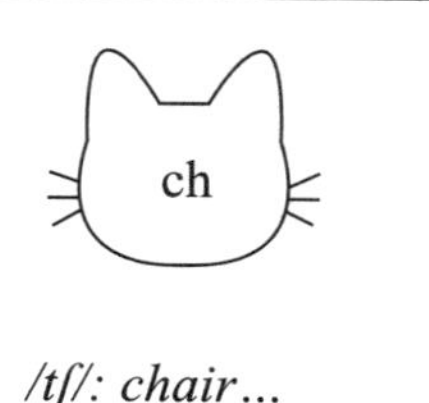

/tʃ/: chair…
/ʃ/: machine…
/k/: school…
/dʒ/: sandwich…

○ 这个游戏中所选取的字母或者字母组合，须有至少两个不同的发音。在第一次玩这个游戏的时候，教师在其中一张海报上可以给出具体的例子，以便学生熟悉规则。

这个游戏的名字为“喂猫咪”，旨在让学生通过小组讨论和竞赛，关注同一字母或者字母组合的不同发音。在这个游戏中，“猫咪”指代的是常见字母或者字母组合，而单词的例子则是“鱼”，学生需要尽可能多地给“猫咪”提供不同种类的“鱼”，即同一个字母或者字母组合的不同发音的例子，从而帮助自己的小组获得更多的分数。

游戏的形式是开放性的，即学生可以在讨论过后，于限定时间内尽可能多地写出例子，通过这样的形式，鼓励所有的同学参与其中。

这个游戏主要用于一阶段的音标复习总结，教师在选择字母或者字母组合时，可以进行适当的归类，帮助学生进行分类复习。以一次 10~15 分钟的游戏为例，可以分为“元音字母在重读开、闭音节中的读音”“部分辅音字母的读音”“部分常见元音字母组合的读音”等不同的专题。比如在“部分常见元音字母组合的读音”这个专题中，就可以出现“ai”“ar”“ay”等元音字母组合。在热闹的游戏过后，教师也要对海报上的字母或字母组合的读音进行总结梳理，帮助学生更加系统地进行识记和复习。

11 Word Stress Maze

Focus: Word Stress

Level: Lower-intermediate

Duration: 5～10 minutes

Procedure:

- Give each student a maze. Tell the students that they are going to find a way out of the maze by following the words that are stressed on the second syllable.

○ 教师可以根据学生的水平更改游戏设定，如寻找重音在第二个音节的三音节单词，以增加游戏难度。

- Individually, the students draw a route by linking the words that are stressed on the second syllable. They can move from one word to another vertically or horizontally but not diagonally. They can't jump over words.
- Check the route together when the students finish.

Sample maze:

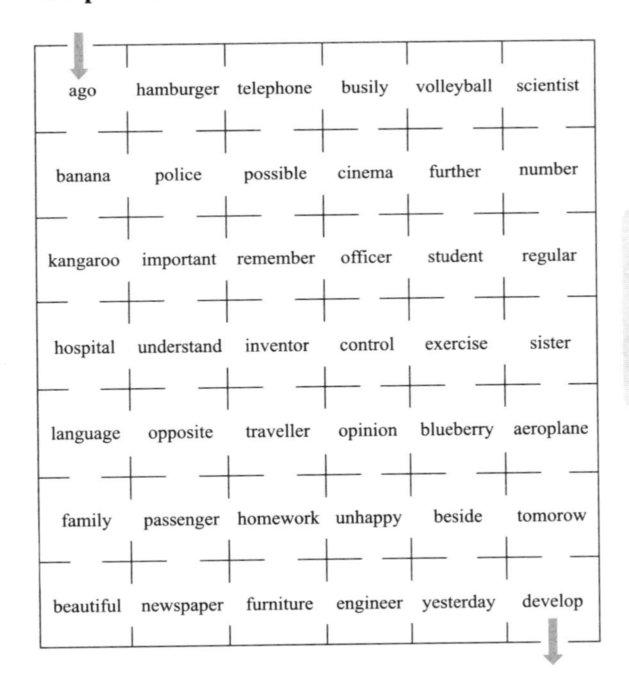

○ 教师在绘制迷宫时，先制作一个网格图，然后选取几个属于同种重音模式的单词，将其填入网格内，形成一条由入口通往出口的连续的、唯一的路线，最后在其他空白网格内填入属于其他重音模式的单词。

这是一个迷宫游戏，名为“单词重音迷宫”。通过这个游戏，可以帮助学生练习识别单词重音。该游戏为单人游戏，学生独自完成，学生需要循着重音在第二个音节的单词的方向走出迷宫，并绘制迷宫的路线图。当然，考虑到学生水平及课堂时间的问题，也可改为两人一组合作完成，降低游戏难度，缩短游戏时间。该游戏兼具了趣味性与实用性，能很好地让学生将注意力集中于单词重音的识别上。另外，该游戏还具有很大的灵活性，教师可以通过更改迷宫尺寸、选择不同难易程度的单词等，绘制不同的迷宫，调整游戏的难易度，以适应不同水平的学生。

在游戏结束后，教师可以让学生将所有单词根据单词重音进行分类并尝试总结其规律。对于学生而言，总结单词重音的规律是有难度的，因此，教师可以根据最终想让学生总结出什么样的规律，来决定在迷宫内放入什么样的单词。例如，许多常见的双音节的名词和形容词，重音通常放在第一个音节上；而许多常见的双音节的动词和介词，重音通常放在第二个音节上。为了让学生总结出此规律，教师就应尽可能选择双音节的单词来置于迷宫中，如 sister、number、control、beside 等。又如，多数前缀和后缀不重读，教师就可以放入单词 unhappy、busily 等；合成的名词重音通常在第一个音节，教师就可以放入单词 blueberry、newspaper 等。

英语中单词重音的基本规则有很多，但不绝对，每条规则都只是经验的总结，也有许多例外，甚至是同一个单词，它的英音与美音重读方式也是不同的。所以，教师在教授单词重音规则时，也要向学生传达此理念，既要学会举一反三，也要学会灵活变通。

12 Spot the Differences!

Focus: Awareness of Sentence Stress

Level: Intermediate

Duration: 10～15 minutes

Procedure:

- Present two pictures on the screen and tell students to find the differences between them. Students can just speak out the differences freely if they find them.
- Ask students to listen to a dialogue about the two pictures and mark the sentence stress. Check the answers and tell students some of the stress rules : Stress tends to fall on content words within an utterance. New information

○ 在让学生编写对话之前，先要让学生了解究竟哪些词需要在句子中重读。在听力的这个环节，教师可以逐步引导学生，并逐一解释规律。

tends to receive prominence in a sentence.

- Ask two voluntary groups to make a dialogue about the other differences in the two pictures according to the sample. The rest of the students should pay attention to the stress and raise questions if necessary.

○ 先让两组学生来进行演示的目的是再一次复习巩固所教授的重音规则，为后续的分组活动作示范。

- Give students more pictures and ask them to make dialogues and share in the whole class.

Examples:

Picture A

Picture B

Student A: I have a 'picture of a lady 'sitting in a park.

Student B: I have a picture of a lady, 'too. She's 'reading a book.

Student A: Oh, 'my lady is reading a 'newspaper.

Student B: Next to the lady there's a big 'tree.

Student A: There's a big tree in my picture, 'too.

Student B: There is a 'dog in 'my picture.

Student A: There are 'two dogs in 'mine.

○ 示例中的对话包含了几个句子中重读的规则：1. 实词重读。2. 表示对比、变化、揭示新信息的词，即使是虚词，也需要重读。

（图片及对话摘自百度文库）

这个游戏叫做“大家来找茬儿”，顾名思义，是让学生找出两张图片中的不同之处。当然，游戏的目的在于学生找出不同后，组织对话进行描述，从而体会句子中的重读规律。

一般来说，句子中需要重读的主要是实词，即句子中的动词、名词等，而表示语法关系的虚词或功能词则无需重读。当然，在日常交际中，还需要根据具体的语言环境来进行分析。比如相同的动词或者名词，如果在上文中出现过，下文中紧接着再出现但是不需要强调时，一般不重读；再比如人称代词，一般不重读，但是当表示强调或者对比时，也需要重读。

这个游戏中，通过先让学生观察两幅图片的不同之处，再让学生进行听力练习，标注重读的单词，可以让学生比较直观地了解语境中的重读规律。当他们自己进行对话时，就会注意对话中表示对比、变化、揭示新信息的词，将它们进行重读。这样的方式可能会比单纯的对话操练更加具有实际意义，也让学生在交际中体会并运用了语音规律。

13 Guess the Background Information

Focus: Awareness of Sentence Stress

Level: Upper-intermediate

Duration: 10～15 minutes

Procedure:

- Divide the whole class into several groups.
- Each group gets a card with one sentence and two pieces of different background information on it. Students in the same group should have a discussion and make two dialogues according to the information given. The dialogues they make must include the sentence on the card with different sentence stress to express the implied meaning.
- After preparation, two students from each group take turns to come to the stage and make dialogues in front of the whole class. While performing, they have to emphasize the sentence stress to make themselves clearly understood.

○ 在学生表演时，教师可以将这小组所抽到卡片上的内容在屏幕上呈现，以便其他同学更加有目标性地找出句子中的重音，也降低其他同学猜测的难度。
○ 当学生熟悉这个游戏后，可以逐渐减少呈现卡片上的内容或者不呈现卡片。

- The rest of the students (except their group members) then figure out the different sentence stress and guess the background information. If the student gets the answer right, he/she wins a point for his/her group and the player get a point for his/her group every time. If no one can answer correctly after three rounds, the player can't get any points for his/her group.
- The group which gains the most points can win the game.

Examples:

> The sentence your dialogue should include:
> I want to have dinner with you.
> Background information:
> (1) The man is busy and he is only available at night.
> (2) The man has something important but secret to tell her.

The dialogues students may make:

(1) A: Hey, John. I've booked a seat in your favourite restaurant. Shall we have lunch together?

B: Oh, sorry, dear. I am quite busy these days and I remember that I've told you I want to have 'dinner with you.

A: OK, I see! See you tomorrow evening.

B: See you!

(2) A: Hello, Jane. I've booked a seat in the most famous restaurant. Shall we have dinner together?

B: Fantastic! You mean "The Paradise Kitchen"? Alice also wants to try the food there. Shall we go together?

A: Come on! I want to have dinner with 'you. You know, we have to discuss some details in the project. Maybe we can go there with Alice next time.

B: OK.

这个游戏的名字为"寻找背景信息"，即让学生根据背景信息编写对话、通过对话来猜测背景信息，通过这样的双向活动，理解句子重音的内涵。在这个游戏中，句子的重音就是一个重要的桥梁。在编写对话的过程中，学生需要通过已知的信息来确定说话人的目标，而这个目标就是通过不同的句子重音来达成的；而在听对话猜测背景信息的过程中，学生需要通过仔细听句子重音，来确定说话人想要重点表达的内容，以猜测背后的含义。想要在游戏中尽可能多拿分数赢得胜利，不仅要关注他人在对话中的重音，同时，在编写本组对话时，也要注重用重音来正确传递信息。

通过这个双向活动，学生可以清晰地理解到在交流过程中，不同的句子重音所体现的重点是不同的，不管是表达信息还是接受信息，都应该关注句子的重音。这个游戏还有一个有趣的地方在于，学生可以根据卡片上的信息编写出各种情境下的对话，学生的创造力有时会带来巨大的惊喜。在所有的小组都经过一轮表演后，也可以在全班范围进行投票，选出表达最清晰、最切题的一组对话。

14 Please Correct Me!

Focus: Awareness of Sentence Stress

Level: Upper-intermediate

Duration: 10～15 minutes

Procedure:

- The teacher invites a volunteer to set an example:
  (1) The volunteer reads the sentence on the card loudly.
  (2) The teacher retells the sentence but replaces one key word on purpose.
  (3) The volunteer repeats the sentence to correct the teacher, especially emphasizing on the replaced word.
  (4) Check for several rounds till the teacher gets the correct sentence.
- Two students pair up into one group. Play this game in each group according to the cards given by the teacher.

○ 教师可以事先准备一些有趣的且包含各类信息的句子让学生进行对话。

Examples:

Volunteer: Mario bought a dog yesterday.
Teacher: Ahh, 'Mary bought a dog yesterday.
Volunteer: 'Mario bought a dog yesterday.
Teacher: Ahh, Mario bought a 'frog yesterday.
Volunteer: Mario bought a 'dog yesterday.
Teacher: Ahh, Mario 'stole a dog yesterday.
Volunteer: Mario 'bought a dog yesterday.
Teacher: Oh, Mario bought a dog yesterday.
Volunteer: Congratulation! You got it!

这个游戏的名字为“请纠正我”，旨在让学生通过不断地强调句中的各类信息，来体会句子重音在交际中的重要性。

游戏的载体就是一个句子，包含时间、地点、人物、具体动作等信息。当第一位学生说完这句话后，第二位学生要尽可能地从不同角度来混淆信息；而第一位学生为了让句中的信息被准确传达，则需要根据第二位学生的复述，及时调整句子的重音，以强调这部分信息。

这个游戏的乐趣在于学生所有的交流都是有明确目的的，真实的。通过不断的复述和纠正，学生会自然地根据语境和目标，调整句子的重音。通过这个活动，学生可以清晰地理解句子重音在交际中的作用。

15 Find My Partner!

Focus: Awareness of Linking Sounds

Level: Low-intermediate

Duration: 10～15 minutes

Procedure:

- Select ten volunteers and divide the rest students into four groups.
- Ten volunteers go forward to the stage area in the front of the classroom. Each of them is randomly given a card with one word prepared by the teacher in advance.
- The volunteers are required to find their partners with the help of the rest students by connecting two words that end and start with the same consonant on the cards.
- After all the volunteers find their partners and form the five phrases, the students in the audience are encouraged to read the phrases. Those who read the phrases correctly can win a point for his/her group.
- After all the five phrases are read correctly, the teacher guides the students to sum up the rules. Those who contribute some useful thoughts or correct rules can win two points for his/ her group.
- The group with the highest points is the winner.

○ 在寻找规律的过程中，任何有价值的正确思考都应该被肯定，以此来鼓励更多的学生参与其中。

Examples:

bus / station
short / time
big / group
hard / day
black / kite

○ 这个游戏中所选取的单词，须符合“同音合并”的规律，即前一个单词词尾辅音和后一个单词词首辅音相同。

这个游戏的名字为“找朋友”，旨在让学生通过具象的活动，主动发现连读中“同音合并”的规律，而不是被动地、机械地接受和记忆规律。在这个游戏中，“找”并不是难点，但是通过“找”这个过程，可以帮助学生直观地发现“同音合并”这个规律适用于哪种情况。

这个游戏主要分为三步：台上学生找到词首与词尾相同的单词，组成词组；台下学生朗读词组；所有学生共同寻找规律。教师在实施这个游戏的过程中，要注重调动班级同学共同参与。比如当台上的同学在“找朋友”的时候，允许台下的同学进行讨论，这在一定程度上也促进了台下同学的思考。另外，教师要鼓励学生勇敢地读出词组，即使有错误，也没有关系，反而是有价值的课堂生成，更有助于引导学生逐步揭示规律。

16 Five-in-a-row

Focus: Awareness of Linking Sounds

Level: Intermediate

Duration: 10～15 minutes

Procedure:

- Prepare the game board in advance and stick it onto the blackboard.
- Divide the whole class into two groups and provide different color pencils for each group.
- Students in each group take turns to choose the phrase in the circle and read it. Color the circle if they read the phrase correctly.
- The winner is the first group to get an unbroken line of five circles. The line can go in any direction: horizontally, vertically, or diagonally.
- The teacher guides the students to analyze the phrases on the blackboard again and conclude the rules.

○ 在游戏开始前，教师可以根据自己的教学目标和重点，强调学生在读词组时需要注意的方面。比如在这个例子中，教师需要提醒学生，只有注意到了连读，才算读正确。

○ 教师可以在游戏结束后，引导学生再次仔细分析这些词组的特点，归纳本节课中的连读规则。

Examples:

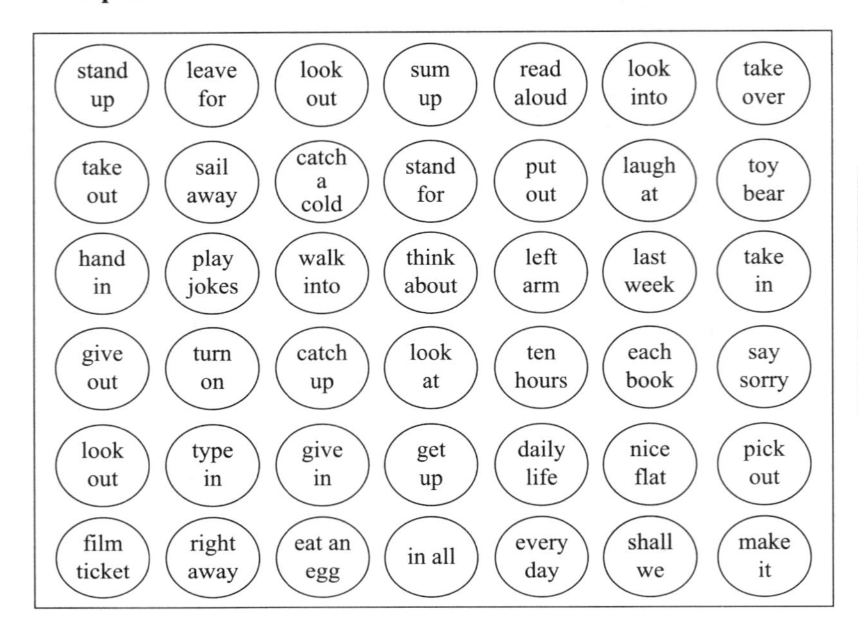

○ 这个示例着重于“辅音词尾+元音词首”的连读规则。教师也可以根据自己的教学目标和重点，设计棋盘里面的内容。

这个游戏可以称之为“语音五子棋”，旨在通过小组间的竞赛，促使学生思考怎样正确读出词组或者句子。教师在游戏结束后可以引导学生归纳总结读音规则。

学生对围棋五子棋的规则可能都有一定的了解，要想赢得这个游戏，学生就必须阻止对方小组率先连成一线。换言之，学生必须将对方小组的目标词组读对，才能为本组争取更大的赢面。比起教师给出示例让学生机械地操练，这个游戏的优点在于通过“五子棋”这个框架，促使学生主动地思考与挑战。

这个示例主要侧重的是连读的规则。连读主要分为两大类，一类是前词的词尾辅音与后词的词首元音相拼，产生连读；另一类是前词的词尾和后词的词首都是元音或辅音，则会互相影响，发生失爆、省音、加音等语音变化。在示例的棋盘中，大部分的例子都符合连读中“辅音词尾+元音词首”的连读规则，其中也有一些不需要连读的例子，这就要求学生进行甄别和思考。在最后归纳总结的环节，教师可以将其中的例子进行对比，让学生更快速地找出规律。

“语音五子棋”这个游戏适用于任何有关读音规则和节奏的操练，在这个框架之下，教师可以通过改变棋盘里面的内容，突出教学重点，达成教学目标。

What Is Missing

Focus: Awareness of Linking Sounds

Level: Upper-intermediate

Duration: 10～15 minutes

Procedure:

- Find an English song and replace some specific words with blanks. These replaced words can be read in succession according to certain rules.
- With the lyrics presented on the screen, students have to figure out the missing words while enjoying the song.
- Volunteers from each group take turns to speak out the answers. Those who fill in the blanks correctly can win one point for his/her group.
- After checking the answers, students then study the missing words again and try to figure out the certain rules. Those who provide valuable answers can win one point for his/her group.
- The group which gains the most points can win the game and they have the right to choose a favorite English song to be played in the next class.

Examples:

Big Big Girl

I'm a big big girl
in a big big world
It's not a big big thing if you leave me
But I do do feel
that I too too will miss you much
miss you much

○ 示例中所选择的歌曲指向的是“词尾辅音＋词首元音”连读，教师也可以根据不同的教学目标和重点，选取不同的歌曲。

这个游戏叫做“缺了什么”，有点类似于近些年比较流行的“我爱填歌词”游戏，旨在让学生通过听歌、填词、研究所填词的特征等一系列活动，熟悉并了解英语连读的规则。

连读对于非母语学生来说是一个难点，它是英语口语的一个重要特点，也是影响学生英语听力和口语水平的一个重要因素，所以在教学中帮助学生理解连读的概念非常有必要。英语歌曲是听力素材之一，朗朗上口的歌谣更能吸引学生的注意。在这个游戏中，教师所要做的就是寻找不同的歌曲素材并研究这首歌曲中所涉及的连读规则。通常在一首歌曲中，可能会包括不同的连读规则，教师可以在一开始时只侧重其中一种进行填空和讲解，再逐渐增加难度。

这个游戏中加入了音乐的元素，不仅可以让学生学习到连读规律，也可以让学生感受其中的节奏、韵律，对于语言学习有一定的帮助。

18 Quick Reaction

Focus: Awareness of Intonation

Level: Lower-intermediate

Duration: 10～15 minutes

Procedure:

- Select twenty volunteers and ask them to stand in a circle.
- The teacher gives instructions with different intonations. For instance, “Touch your nose.” “Shake your head.” etc.
- Students should quickly react after hearing the instruction. For example, if the teacher says “Touch your nose.” with a falling tone, the students should touch their noses quickly. On the contrary, if the teacher gives the instruction with a rising tone, the students should stay still.
- If the student reacts improperly, he/she will be out. The one who stands in the circle till the end wins the game.

○ 当台上的学生在参与游戏时，其余学生可以作为观察者，帮助教师指出哪位同学做出了错误的反应或者动作。

Examples:

Touch your nose. ↗

Shake your head. ↗

Clap your hands. ↘

Nod your head. ↘

这个游戏名为“快速反应”，旨在让学生通过正确判断和快速反应，了解语调在交流中的重要性。游戏的规则很简单：学生通过判断教师所读指令的语调，来确定是否做出相应的动作。在这个游戏中，所有的指令都是祈使句，只有当教师用降调来发出指令时，学生才需要做出相应的动作。游戏既考验了学生的判断力和反应力，也向学生传达了这样的信息：在交流中，我们需要运用正确的语调来达成自己说话的意图。

19 Telephone Conversation

Focus: Awareness of Intonation

Level: Intermediate

Duration: 10～15 minutes

Procedure:

- Select twenty volunteers and ask them to line up in two groups, 10 volunteers in each group.
- The teacher gives a note with a sentence of the certain intonation to the first student in each group.
- The first student whispers the sentence to the second student. One by one, the last student in each group speaks out the sentence aloud.
- The teacher posts the two notes on the screen and all the students can check whether the last student correctly retells the sentence with the certain intonation.
- The students then discuss the inner meaning of each sentence in the telephone conversation.

Examples:

(1) Our English teacher said we would go for a spring outing next Thursday. ↘

Our English teacher said we would go for a spring outing next Thursday? ↗

○ 这个示例中的第一句话为陈述事实，第二句话则表达了惊讶、怀疑。

(2) A: We will have a picnic at 9:00 a.m. this Sunday. ↘

B: What time? ↗

A: We will go for a picnic this Sunday. ↘

B: What time? ↘

○ 这个示例中用升调说 what time, 表示没有听清对方所说话语中的信息，要求对方重复；用降调说 what time 则是正常询问具体时间。

这个游戏叫做“传声筒”，旨在让学生通过倾听、模仿句子的语调，理解句子所要表达的意图和态度。

每一轮游戏通常由两组学生来完成，最后呈现的是两个相同的句子，但是语调则不同。当每组最后一名学生大声说出句子后，教师要在屏幕上呈现两个小组所拿到的纸条。学生不仅要核对这两个小组是否正确运用了语调，还要对比、讨论这两句话的不同含义。

这个游戏虽然没有胜负，但是参与度很广。参与游戏的学生可以在倾听、模仿的过程中体会语调的重要性；参与讨论的学生可以通过对比、讨论来理解不同语调所表达的意思，从而进一步了解正确使用语调在交际中的重要性。

20 We're Poets

Focus: Rhyme in the Poems

Level: Advanced

Duration: 10～15 minutes

Procedure:

- Prepare several poems with different rhyme. Assign one poem sheet to each group.

- Students in the groups should analyze the assigned poem and find out the words with rhyme.
- Imitate a poem and write it down on a poster.
- Make a class presentation in groups.

○ 仿写和朗读展示需要更多的时间准备，教师可以在布置任务后，给学生充足的时间进行准备。

Examples:

The Elephant

The elephant is surely grand!
It's the largest creature on land!
With jumbo-sized ears,
No wonder it hears
For miles from where it may stand.

The elephant is surely great!
Over five tons is its weight!
With jumbo-sized feet,
Plus a mouth that can eat
More than 700 pounds on its plate.

The elephant is surely strong!
With ivory tusks sharp and long!
And the heaviest chunk
It can lift with its trunk!
Yes, and elephant just can't go wrong!

（选自印度期刊 *Rejoice*）

Possible verse:

The Mice

The mice are surely disgusting!
With small faces and ears,
They nibble things they shouldn't touch.
And no one seems to like them very much.

这个游戏名为“我们是诗人”，旨在让学生通过欣赏诗歌、找出押韵词、仿写诗歌等活动，感受诗歌的韵律。

在语音学习中，朗读童谣或者诗歌，识别其中的韵律也是一项内容。这个游戏以一些内容符合学生认知、韵律朗朗上口的诗歌为载体，让学生通过小组合作，找出押韵词，并仿写诗歌，进行朗读展示。在识别押韵词和仿写的过程中，学生需要结合所学过的音标知识才能完成各项任务，因此这是一个很好的复习音标的方式。同时，小组朗读诗歌进行展示的过程，也需要学生注意诗歌的韵律、节奏等，在潜移默化中感受诗歌韵律之美。

这个游戏虽然没有胜负之分，也无需进行小组间的竞争，但是它的魅力在于学生对诗歌进行了研究后，仿写诗歌并展示的过程。在课堂上，教师可以利用 10~15 分钟的时间带领学生分析诗歌；而后，教师可以在班级中利用一周的时间开展诗歌展示活动，比如将学生的诗歌海报贴在教室外墙进行投票比拼，举行英语诗歌朗读大赛等，以鼓励学生积极参与，营造共同欣赏诗歌之美的氛围。

Part Two

Vocabulary
（词汇）

21 Funny Wheels

Focus: Prefixes and Suffixes

Level: Beginner to Lower-intermediate

Duration: 8～10 minutes

Procedure:

- Before the activity, make a copy of the card for each pair of learners in the class. See as below:
  (1) Draw two wheels of the same size on the card.
  (2) Write the prefix (e.g. un-) on the top wheel and root words (e.g. happy, friendly, etc.) on the bottom wheel.
  (3) Cut out the "window" on the top wheel（shown in the picture）.
  (4) Fix the two wheels with a spin. Make sure they spin freely.
- Learners spin the wheel to form a new word.
- For beginners, they need to read the new word correctly；for learners of lower-intermediate proficiency or above, they need to make a sentence by using the new word they've formed.

Examples:

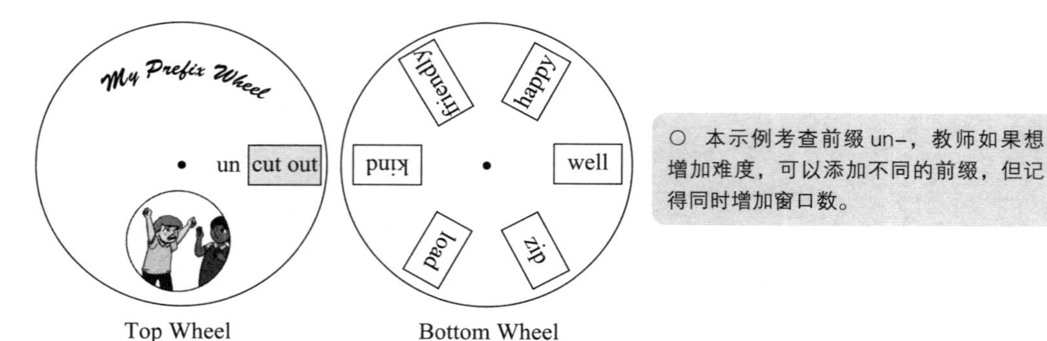

Top Wheel　　Bottom Wheel

这个游戏叫做“趣味转盘”，可以用来帮助学生巩固对派生词的掌握。活动前，教师要准备好满足学习小组需求数量的转盘道具。学习者转动转盘，配对形成一个新的单词。对于初学者，要求学生能正确识读新生成的单词；对于有一定基础的学生，还可以要求他们用新生成的单词造句。此外，教师也可以升级转盘，增加不同的词缀来提高配对的难度。“趣味转盘”的使用是很灵活的，示例中所展示的是对前缀的考查，教师还可以将它设计成后缀、可数名词的复数、形容词的比较级等其他内容。

这个游戏简单轻松，可在不同场景使用，学生可以在家独自进行游戏，自查对知识的掌握程度；也可以在课堂内进行小组活动，组员们一起探讨同一词根可以有哪些不同的词缀。

22 Flipping & Matching

Focus: Capital Cities

Level: Beginner

Duration: 10 minutes

Procedure:

- Before the activity, teacher makes a copy of cards for each pair in the class. On every card printed the name of a country or its capital.
- Two learners work as a group. Before the game, place all the cards face down, and make sure neither players can see the words on the cards.
- The two players take turns to flip the cards, two cards at a time.
- If the two cards don't go with each other, the player must put them back right where they were with face down. Then the other player gets the opportunity to flip.

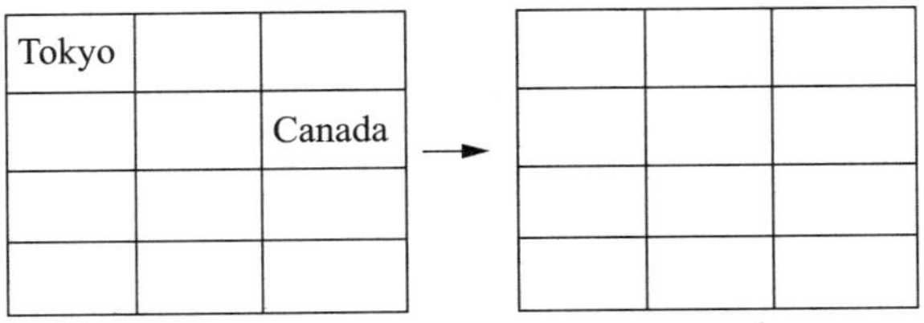

Tokyo		
		Canada

→

○ 教师在制作卡片时可以大胆地添加一些课外词汇，如 Denmark（丹麦）和 Copenhagen（哥本哈根）。因为很多国家和首都的英文表达与中文译音接近。

e.g. The player gets *Tokyo* and *Canada*. Tokyo is not the capital of Canada. Then the player must put the cards back.

- If the two cards go with each other correctly, the player can keep both cards. Then the other player continues to flip another two cards among the rest...

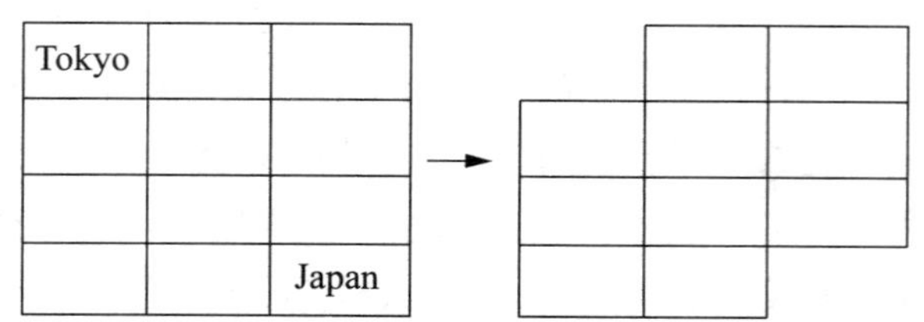

e.g. The player gets Tokyo and Japan. Tokyo is the capital of Japan. The player can take both cards.

Examples:

Tokyo	Bangkok	Wellington
Rome	Washington	Italy
New Zealand	America	Toronto
Thailand	Canada	Japan

Keys:

Bangkok-Thailand, Wellington-New Zealand, Rome-Italy, Toronto-Canada, Tokyo-Japan, Washington-America

该游戏叫做“转一转，配一配”，是一个单词配对游戏，适合个人或小组内进行。上文示例演示了如何使用该游戏对国家和首都相关词汇进行训练。

《上海市初中英语学科教学基本要求》一书中指出初中阶段学生需掌握America, Australia, Britain, Canada, China, France, Germany, Italy, Japan 等国家的英文表达。在《牛津英语（上海版）》6BU1 中，出现了 Beijing，Tokyo，Bangkok 三个亚洲重要首都城市，在 7BU3 中出现了加拿大首都 Toronto，以上都是学生需要掌握的。此外，英语是一门交际语言，在实际生活中，掌握或基本了解重要国家和首都的英文表达对学生而言是非常必要的。因此，教师们可以通过这个游戏，给学生们多拓展一些国家和首都的英文表达，让学生在游戏中掌握这些单词。

这个游戏不仅适用于训练国家和首都名称，事实上，它也可以被灵活地运用于操练近义词、反义词、短语动词等。比如，在考查 phrasal verb（短语动词）时，教师可以设计一些卡片诸如 *call on* 和 *visit*，*go into* 和 *enter* 等。

23 Lantern Riddles

Focus: Nouns

Level: Beginner

Duration: 30 minutes

Procedure:

- Teacher prints riddles on slips of colored paper and attaches them to the bottom of lanterns.
- In the classroom, hang the lanterns at the proper height for students to read and guess the riddles.
- Students walk around in the classroom to read the riddles, ponder and figure out the solutions.
- When the students come up with the solutions to the riddles, they can pull the paper out and go to the teacher to check the answers. They will get one point for each correct solution.
- After the game, teacher can give students little gifts according to the points they get.

○ 对于难度较大的灯谜，可在谜题下附提示，指明谜底的类别，如食物、日用品、国家名称等。

Examples:

Samples of riddles:

（1）What belongs to you but others use it more than you do?

（2）It works hard all its life, counting numbers day and night, but never gets past 12. What is it?

（3）What gets wetter and wetter the more it dries?

（4）What building has the most stories?

（5）They look like twin brothers, both sturdy and tall. They work together and

○ 本例谜底均为中考考纲词汇，仅供参考，教师可根据课上要操练的名词自定义谜面。

go everywhere together. But they only go near solid food and do not care for soup. Who are they?

（6）He devotes his life to looking after the house. His mate always follows when the master goes out. A gentleman sees him and goes away. A villain sees him and it spells bad luck. Who is he?

（7）Use the 10 letters 'acdhijlnp' to spell out the names of three Asian countries. Each name must be five letters long, and the three countries must be neighbors.

Keys:

（1）Name （2）Clock （3）Towel （4）Library （5）Chopsticks （6）Lock （7）China, Japan, India

该游戏叫做"猜灯谜"，旨在帮助学生通过有趣的猜谜游戏来巩固词汇。词汇分为实词和虚词两大类，掌握较多的实词是提高文章阅读能力的关键，而名词作为实词中最为重要的词类，值得教师们重点关注。日常教学中，我们可以通过一些小游戏来丰富学生学习名词的体验，帮助他们更好地强化对名词的记忆与理解。

谜题除由教师设计之外，不妨让学生自己尝试撰写，学生在设计灯谜时必然要先完全弄清单词的含义，这不失为另一种巩固词汇的手段。

24 Super Brain

Focus: Prepositions

Level: Beginner

Duration: 30 minutes

Procedure:

- Bring a toy and a box to the class. Put the toy in different positions of the box and ask the class to describe where it is.

  e.g. Peppa pig is in the box.

  Peppa pig is beside the box.

- Encourage the class to brainstorm the words to describe position as many as possible.

  e.g. in, on, at, beside, above, below, in front of, opposite, etc.

- Put several photos on the teacher's desk. Ask each pair to come to front to pick one.
- In pair, learners try to describe the photo by using prepositions.

  e.g. A sailing boat is on the sea.

  A toy shovel is next to the sandcastles.

  A starfish is on the sand.

  A boy is sitting under the parasol.

  Some seagulls are flying above the sea.

  Some clouds are wandering in the sky.

- Split the class into groups of 3~4 and give each group a picture.
- The group have one minute to observe the picture. Then they take turns to tell where every item is placed without looking at the picture.
- The player who cannot tell is out. The one who stands last wins the game.

该游戏叫做“最强大脑”，旨在帮助学生练习正确使用介词来表达物体所在的位置。介词作为表达地点、方位的专用词，具有不可或缺的意义。理解介词的词义、掌握介词的搭配，在英语词汇学习中尤为重要。

游戏通过让学生观察图片，回忆图片中物件摆放位置，使学生在记忆挑战中，巩固对介词词义的理解与运用。

在介词的词汇教学中，一词多义也是教学重点之一。比如，介词 with 可以表示“带有，具有”，也可以表示“以，用”，还可以表示“和……一起”等不同的含义。教师同样可以使用本游戏帮助学生巩固介词的一词多义。比如，让学生观察以下图片，并要求他们用 with 来描述图片信息。

Possible answers:

George is having breakfast with his family.

They are having food with spoons.

The lady with long, warped eyelashes is George's mom.

25 Making Tracks

Focus: Word Class (adjectives & adverbs ended with-ly)

Level: Beginner

Duration: 20 minutes

Procedure:

- Write two lists of words on the board. Ask what parts of speech they are.

  (1) carefully, warmly, politely

  (2) friendly, lovely, manly
- Point out that not all the words ended with-ly are adverbs. They can also be adjectives. Then explain that some words can be either adjectives or adverbs

(see below). And ask them if they can name more examples and write the words on the board.

Adjectives	Adverbs
daily newspapers	publish daily
monthly salary	exercise monthly
lively boy	step lively
the nightly skies	appear nightly

- Split the class into pairs. Give each pair a board and a dice. Tell them the rules on how to play the game.

  (1) To win the game, the player must get more points than the other. And to win points, they must make a track. (Note: A track is a straight line of four or more squares. The track can be horizontal, vertical or diagonal.)

  (2) Players take turns to throw the dice and win squares. If the dice shows 1 or 4, the player can win any square with the word that can only be adjectives. If the dice shows 2 or 5, the player can win any square with the word that only be adverbs. If the dice shows 3 or 6, the player can win any square with the word that be either adjectives or adverbs. When the player wins a square, he/she can draw a typical symbol in it. For example, one can use the symbol ○ and then the other can use the symbol ×.

  (3) When all the squares are full, count the points! Four points for every track of four squares, five points for every track of five square and six points for every track of six squares. The player who gets more points wins!

Examples:

daily	automatically	lately	quietly	deeply	actively
curly	widely	lively	truly	deadly	elderly
hardly	warmly	unlikely	politely	fully	lonely
smelly	quarterly	highly	angrily	monthly	quickly
nightly	possibly	carelessly	wisely	sadly	friendly
cowardly	energetically	costly	lovely	homely	closely

形容词：costly, curly, elderly, unlikely, lonely, smelly, friendly, deadly, lovely

副词：lately, quietly, deeply, actively, widely, truly, hardly, warmly, politely, fully, highly, angrily, quickly, possibly, carelessly, wisely, sadly, cowardly, automatically, energetically, closely

既可作形容词也可作副词：daily, quarterly, monthly, lively

这个游戏叫做“找一找，连一连”，适合用来强化易混淆词的区分。在本示例中，主要是对 -ly 结尾的单词做词性的辨析。

在词汇学习中，形容词、副词都是非常重要的 descriptive word（描述性词），用好形容词、副词对学生的口语表达和写作都有好处。但是，不少学生会盲目地将所有 -ly 结尾的单词都认作副词，因此在使用中产生了不恰当的表述。本设计就是让学生通过游戏来巩固常见的 -ly 结尾的单词，区分这些高频单词中哪些是形容词、副词，哪些既可作形容词亦可作副词。

教师也可以用这个游戏来巩固其他单词，甚至可以用在语音学习中，比如区分单音节、双音节和多音节等。

26 Growing Number

Focus: Numeral Words

Level: Elementary

Duration: 8～10 minutes

Procedure:

- Write the following numbers on the board and ask the class to try to read them.

  128 = one hundred and twenty-eight

  211 = two hundred and eleven

  609= six hundred and nine

- Explain the rule of how to read large numbers.

  100,000 = one hundred thousand

  100,000,000 = one hundred million

  100,000,000,000 = one hundred billion

- Help the leaners to practice reading before the game starts.

  128,000 = one hundred and twenty-eight thousand

  211,128,000 = two hundred and eleven million, one hundred and twenty-eight thousand

  609,211,128,000 = six hundred and nine billion, two hundred and eleven million, one hundred and twenty-eight thousand
- Split the class into groups of three or four, and each group gets one dice. (Note: A normal dice can work, but it would be better if you can make a special dice with numbers from zero to nine on it.)
- Players take turns rolling the dice and adding numbers to the one already on the paper, watching the number "snake" growing with each turn.
- The number becomes longer and players must read the entire number. Make sure each person gets at least three turns.
- By the end of the game, the players will be reading a number at least as long as 111,111,111,111.

该游戏叫做“变大的数字”，旨在帮助学生训练大数字的读法。在日常教学中常常会发现，即使是能够流利地朗读或表达整个句子的同学，每当遇到数字时也常会出现卡顿的情况，无法及时反应过来。而在听力训练中，对数字的反应不够迅速又导致学生更易失分。因此，推荐老师们使用该游戏帮助学生对数字的读法进行巩固训练。

需要注意的是，英语中会用逗号把数字分隔成每三位一组，教师可以先训练学生三位数以下的数字读法，在学生了解规律后，就能轻松读出大数字了。

27 Join the Dots

Focus: Word Category

Level: Lower-intermediate

Duration: 15 minutes

Procedure:

- Write the following sentences on the board. Ask students to judge which one is correct or incorrect.

  (√) A pony is smaller than a horse.

  (×) Jack performs more perfect than Eddie.
- Elicit or explain that non-gradable adjectives are those do not occur in comparative or superlative forms because we don't imagine degrees of more or less of the quality being described.
- Give each student or each pair a worksheet. Ask them to find out the non-gradable adjectives and join the dots.
- Once they complete the work, they will find out what the whole picture is like. It would be fun!

Examples:

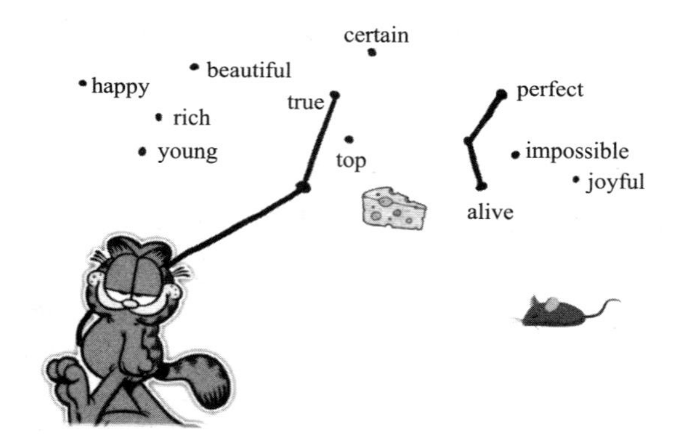

○ 学生需找出图中非等级形容词，并将它们连接起来。

Keys:

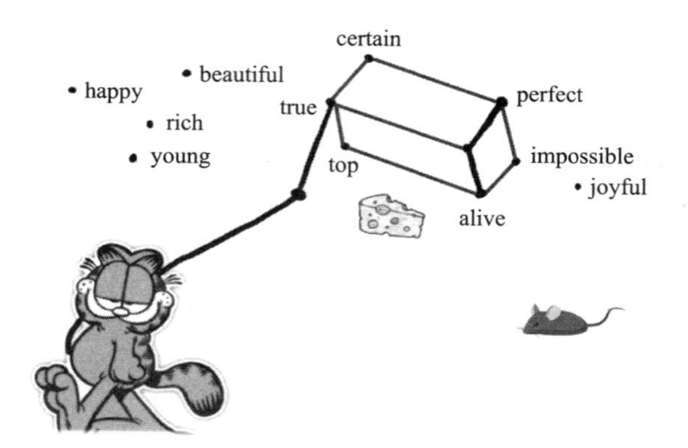

○ 正确连接所有非等级形容词，就能还原出完整图片。

这个游戏叫“连连看”，适用于低年级学生进行词汇分类的训练。如以上示例中，设计意图是让学生区分等级和非等级形容词。教师也可以根据自身教学需求，设计其他内容，如区分及物动词和不及物动词、可数名词和不可数名词等。该游戏可由学生独立完成，或小组内两两合作完成。

教师在活动前要准备好连连看的素材，选择具有一定趣味性的图片，并将目标单词设计在图片相应的轨迹上。游戏的步骤为：学生按要求找出相应的单词，并将这些单词用线连接起来，最后就能还原出完整的图片。

28 Win a Word

Focus: Compounds

Level: Lower-intermediate

Duration: 15 minutes

Procedure:

- Split the class into groups of five and give each group a set of cards. Each group chooses one player as the dealer. The dealer is responsible for giving the cards.

○ 每组拿 A、B 两副牌，A 牌由发牌者持有，B 牌由四位玩家摸牌持有。A、B 两副牌面的单词能构成合成词。

- For the first round, the four players take turns to draw five cards. Once the dealer gives a card, the players need to find out one card which can go with it to make up a compound word.

○ 发牌者每出一张卡片，四位玩家要迅速反应，看手中的卡片是否能和给出的卡片构成合成词。最先打出合理卡片的玩家，可以一并赢走台面上的两张卡片，并继续摸牌，以此类推。

- The player who gives the correct card can have both cards.
- The game ends when cards are run out. The winner is the person with the most cards at the end of the play.

Examples:

The dealer gives a card *every*. The four players take turns to give a card which can go with *every*. For example, one player gives a card *day*. *Every* and *day* can make up a new compound word *everyday*. Then the player can take both cards *every* and *day*. Skip the round if two cards cannot be made into a compound word.

该游戏叫做“赢卡片”，旨在帮助学生巩固对合成词的理解。合成法是最为常见的构词法之一，在《上海市初中英语学科教学基本要求》一书中提到，中学生需要能识别并理解由合成法构成的单词，而该游戏则可让学生在趣味游戏中学习合成词。

合成词亦称复合词，指的是由两个或两个以上单词构成的英语单词。从书写的角度看，合成词共有三种写法：open compounds (ice cream), closed compounds (doorknob) 和 hyphenated compounds (long-term)；而从词性的角度看，则有合成名词 (football)、合成形容词 (peace-loving)、合成动词 (outact)、合成副词 (whole-heartedly) 等。因此，教师在设计卡片上的单词时，需要考虑好本节课要训练哪些词汇。

通过这个游戏，学生能更好地掌握复合词构词法知识，大大提高记忆单词的效率。而且，在阅读中他们也可以通过构词法知识来分解单词、破解词意，消除阅读障碍，提高阅读理解能力。

29 From A to Z

Focus: Sports

Level: Lower-intermediate

Duration: 40 minutes

Procedure:

- Write the alphabets from A to Z on the board and ask the class to stand in a straight line. If you have a large class, you can split them into different groups.
- The class take turns to rush to the board to write a sport starts with a certain letter. The one who cannot think of a sport knocks out.
- After the game, you will have a whole list of sports on the board. Be cautious if there are any sport your learners don't know, explain it to them. Or you can ask the learner who wrote that word to explain to the class.

Examples:

A- archery, artistic gymnastics, artistic swimming

B- badminton, baseball, basketball, beach volleyball, biathlon, bobsleigh, bowling, boxing, bull riding

C- canoeing, cheerleading, climbing, cricket, cross country skiing, curling, cycling

D- diving, discus, dodgeball

E- equestrian, esports (electronic gaming)

F- field hockey, figure skating, fishing, Formula 1, fencing

G- golf, gymnastics

H- handball, high jump, horse racing, hurdle

I- ice hockey, ice skating,

J- javelin, judo

K- karate, kickball

L- lacrosse, long jump, luge

M- marathon, mixed martial arts (MMA), modern pentathlon, motoGP, mountain biking

N- NASCAR, nordic combined

O- Olympic diving, Olympic shooting

P- poker, pole vault, polo (horses), powerlifting

Q- quidditch

R- racquetball, rhythmic gymnastics, road cycling, rowing, rugby

S- sailing, scuba diving, short track, shot put, skateboarding, skiing, snooker, snowboarding, soccer, softball, speed skating, sprinting, surfing, swimming

T- table tennis, taekwondo, tennis, track and field (Athletics), track cycling, trampoline, triathlon, triple jump

U- ultimate frisbee

V- volleyball

W- water polo, weight throw, weightlifting, wrestling

X- XC skiing

Y- yachting, yak polo, yukigassen (snowball fighting)

Z- zorb football

- Show part of a picuture of chess boxing on the screen and let the class guess what sport it is.
- Explain to the class that chess boxing is a hybrid sport, combining playing chess and boxing into a new form. Explain to them that a hybrid sport is one which combines two or more sports in order to create a new sport, or to allow meaningful competition between players of those sports.
- Split the class into groups of four. Ask them to brainstorm a new hybrid sport. And complete the worksheet in groups.
- Learners share their ideas in the class.

Examples:

Design A Sport
Sport Name: Tennis Polo
Number of players: 9 players，1 goalkeeper
Equipment: Racquets
Rules: • Start the game with a jump ball by a referee at midfield. • Players can either kick the ball or hit the ball. • Each player can only keep the ball no more than 5 seconds at a time. • The team hit or kicks the ball into the goal wins 1 point.
Description: • Exciting • Competitive

这个游戏叫做“从 A 到 Z”，教师根据教学目标设定主题，学生围绕该主题，头脑风暴出以 26 个字母开头的相关词汇。游戏中，教师让全班排成一列，轮流到黑板上写出一个特定字母开头的运动，帮助学生巩固运动类名词。

对于高年级的同学，教师还可以进一步开展“设计一项运动”的任务。学生分小组讨论，尝试设计一项混搭的新运动，并在表格中写出运动名称、玩家人数、所需准备和比赛规则等。这项任务既可以进一步巩固学生对运动名词的掌握，也可以锻炼他们的创造性思维。

30 Emotional Board Game

Focus: Feelings

Level: Lower-intermediate

Duration: 40 minutes

Procedure:

- Hand out a work sheet to each pair.
- Learners discuss and match the activities with the possible emotions.

Task 1: Match the activity to the emotions.	
Activity	**Emotion**
Being given a present. Listening to your favorite song. Forgetting your PE kit. Falling over in the playground.	Anxious Upset Excited Happy
Activity	**Emotion**
Meeting a monster. Winning a prize. Having a birthday party. Playing with friends	Happy Excited Scared Proud
Activity	**Emotion**
Eating worms! Watching TV. Being teased. Not being able to sleep.	Tired Disgusted Sad Relaxed

- Ask learners to brainstorm more words about emotional feelings and write them on the board.
- Split the class into groups of 4~6. Allow them to have a fun board game on sharing emotions and stories.
- Players take turns to roll the dice. They need to make a sentence by using the

word where the dice lands. See the example sentence:

e.g. I feel happy when I am riding my bike.

- The first player to get to the end wins.

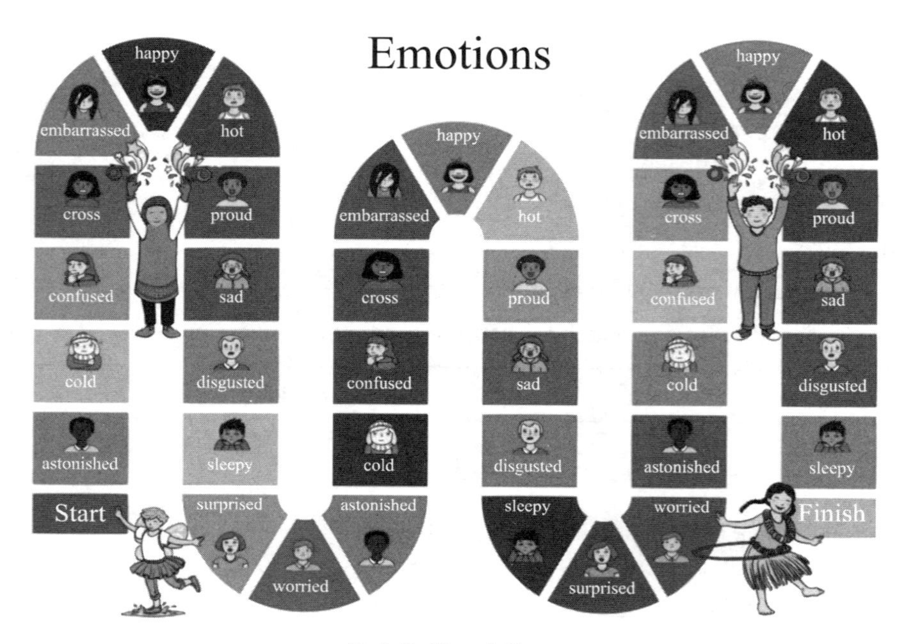

Task 2: Board Game

(https://www.twinkl.com.hk/resource/ma-t-t-253148-emotions-board-game-english-mandarin-chinese)

- After the board game, they will have known each other's feelings in certain situations. They discuss a way out and then complete the work sheet.

Task 3: If I'm feeling... , I can... .		
Name	Feeling	Strategy

e.g. If I'm feeling stressed, I can squeeze my stress ball.

这个游戏叫做“情绪棋盘”，旨在帮助学生在游戏中操练表达情绪的形容词。在引入环节中，教师通过难度较低的连线配对帮助学生热身，回顾一些常见的情绪形容词，接着引导学生们头脑风暴更多的情绪形容词，为后一阶段的练习做准备。

第二部分为核心环节，学生 4~6 人一组开展情绪棋盘游戏，这一阶段老师多旁听，鼓励学生对情绪感受进行更充分的叙述。最后阶段是第二部分的延续。同学们在棋盘游戏中会有正面的情绪，也会有负面的情绪，那么教师可以在最后一个环节引导同学们在小组里讨论如何面对负面情绪。整节课操练了情绪类形容词，同时，还有助于培养学生的社会情绪能力。

31 Bacon's Law

Focus: Lexical Resource

Level: Lower-intermediate

Duration: 30 minutes

Procedure:

- Split the class into different groups. Hand out a deck of word cards and a dice to each group.
- One player picks two cards to get the target words. And then toss the dice. The dice gives a number. This is how many steps the players must use to make connection between the two words.
- The player thinks of words that share similar traits, synonyms, or connector words to move from one term to another in the certain steps.
- If the player succeeds in making the two words connected. He or she can win both two cards. Otherwise, just put the two cards aside.
- The group members take turns to play it. The one who gets most cards in the end is the winner.

○ 教师在制作单词卡片时，可大胆选用相互之间毫不相干的单词，以提升游戏的想象空间，让学生更有挑战的兴趣。

○ 单词卡片正面朝下摆放，玩家抽取最上面的两张，从而获得任务单词；接着投掷骰子，骰子的点数是将两个单词建立联系的最多步骤数。

○ 若玩家在规定步骤内说出合理的单词，使得两个任务单词建立起联系，则本环节胜利，并获得刚才抽到的两张卡片；若玩家无法说出单词，或说出的单词无法合理地将两个任务单词建立联系，则本环节失利，不可获得卡片。

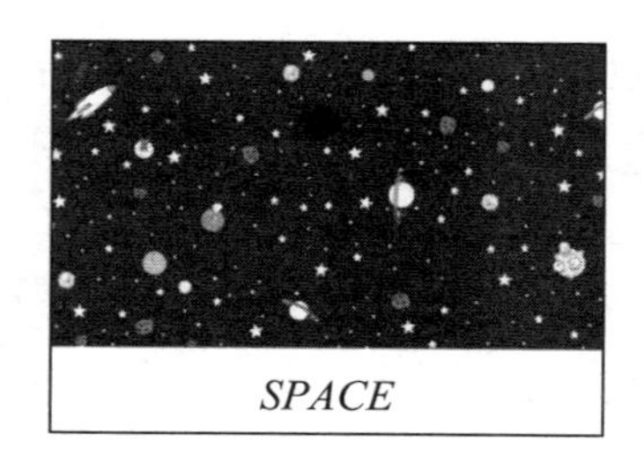
SPACE

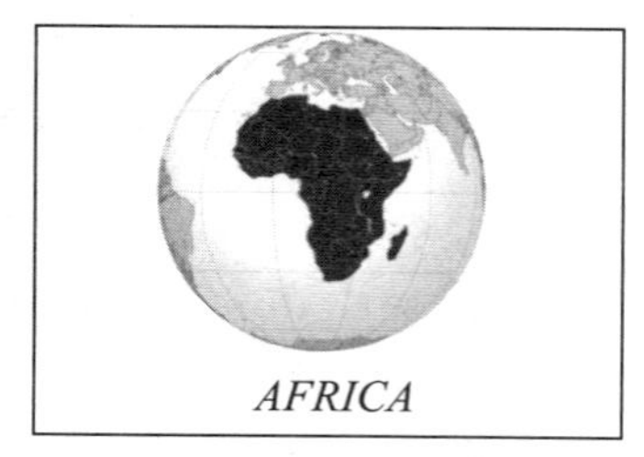
AFRICA

Examples:

The first player picks two word cards. The words he gets are *space* and *Africa* as above. Then he tosses the dice, he gets the number 2. In other words, he has to think of words to connect *space* and *Africa* together within no more than two steps. After thinking for a while, he says *space-solar-heat-Africa*. Well, it makes sense that these words function like a bridge, connecting *space* and *Africa* together. So the player can keep both cards. If the player cannot think of the appropriate words or the words just cannot connect *space* with *Africa* reasonably, then he or she cannot keep either of the two cards.

这个游戏叫做“培根定律”，灵感来自基于“六度分离”理论的凯文·培根客厅游戏，它假定地球上任意两个人都可由至多六个人建立起连结。这个游戏旨在帮助学生针对词汇进行趣味复习。

在英语学习过程中，词汇是非常重要的。对于任何阶段的学生而言，扎实地掌握词汇能极大地提升阅读理解能力。这个游戏丰富了学生背单词的体验，比起单一、枯燥的背诵，学生更乐于在游戏中学习、巩固词汇。此外，学生若对单词的理解越全面，掌握一个单词的多种涵义，则越能胜任这款游戏。因此，对于检测学生对单词的掌握程度，以及是否真正理解单词的不同涵义，这款游戏都是不错的选择！

32 Let’s Compare!

Focus: Comparative & Superlative Degree

Level: Lower-intermediate

Duration: 20 minutes

Procedure:

- Show a slide of pictures and ask the class to choose the correct word in each sentence to add the suffix-er or-est.

Chandler's house is large than Joey's.	My dress is plain than yours.	The waves are rough close to the rocks.

The pig who built his house of bricks was the smart.	Tim's Halloween costume was the scary at the party.	My cupcake was the creamy.

Keys:

Chandler's house is larger than Joey's.

My dress is plainer than yours.

The waves are rougher close to the rocks.

The pig who built his house of bricks was the smartest.

Tim's Halloween costume was the scariest at the party.

My cupcake was the creamiest.

- Hand out a worksheet to each pair. Ask the class to read the story and choose whether each word in bold needs the suffix-er or-est to make sense.

The Hare and the Tortoise

Once upon a time, there was a hare who always bragged about being **fast** than any other animal in the forest. Tired of hearing him boast, the tortoise challenged him, saying "Let's have a race and see who is the **fast**."

Hare was sure that the tortoise was **slow** than him. All the other animals thought that Tortoise would lose because he was known to be the **slow** in the forest.

All the animals in the forest gather to watch the race. Hare ran down the road quickly but soon paused to rest. He thought to himself, "I am the **quick**! There is plenty of time for me to relax!" Tortoise walked and walked. He never stopped until he came to the finish line. The animals who were watching cheered so loudly for Tortoise, they woke up Hare. Hare stretched and yawned and began to run again, but it was too late. Tortoise was over the line. Although Hare was **quick** than Tortoise, Tortoise knew that he was **steady** than Hare.

Keys: faster; fastest; slower; slowest; quickest; quicker; steadier

这个游戏叫做“我们比一比”，旨在训练学生对形容词的比较级和最高级的正确使用。第一个环节通过图片让学生直观地感受两个事物间如何用比较级进行比较。第二个环节通过生动的故事，让学生对比较级和最高级的运用场景有了更好的了解。这个游戏由浅入深地加强了学生对形容词比较级和最高级的理解。

33 What's in the Box?

Focus: Descriptive Words

Level: Lower-intermediate

Duration: 15 ～ 20 minutes

Procedure:

- Before the activity, prepare a non-transparent box or you can cover it with cloth, in case players see the items inside while playing the game.
- Prepare some items to put in the box. Common objects in daily life would be nice because it won't be too hard for players to guess. Choose items of

different materials, shapes, sizes, etc., so that more adjectives can be used to describe the items during the game. Drop the items in the box and mix them up.

- Now we can start the game! Have one player come up to the front and put his/her hand in to find an item. Don't forget to tell them not to bring out the item!
- Have the player describe the item he/she touches by using adjectives or any other descriptive word and let the rest of the students guess. (Note: If you have younger learners or learners of low proficiency, you can show a selection of words they could use on the screen, or even a list of the items in the box as well.)
- Keep going until all the items have been found!

Examples:

Item suggestions:

Articles of daily use: battery, blanket, mirror, plate, scarf, soap, wallet...

Groceries: tomato, chips, corn, dumpling, garlic, peach, pepper, pineapple...

Stationaries & tools: eraser, pencil-case, map, dictionary, hammer...

Digital products: camera, keyboard, cell phone, mouse (of a computer)...

> ○ 这些单词都属于初中学段考核范围，且都是学生生活中常见的物件，比较适合学生描述和猜测，教师也可以酌情加大难度。

Descriptive words suggestions:

Two dimensional shapes: triangle, circle, semi-circle, oval, square, rectangle, parallelogram, etc.

Three dimensional shapes: cube, cuboid, cone, etc.

Texture: hard, soft, rough, smooth, dark, light, etc.

Materials: ribbon, metal, wood, lace, leather, sand, etc.

Sizes: big, small, long, short, tall, huge, tiny, etc.

Adjectives: beautiful, bright, concrete, handy, luxurious, organic, ordinary, etc.

> ○ 这里有一部分单词虽然不在考核范围，但却是实际生活中有高需求的单词，教师可以酌情补充，以供学生操练。

该游戏叫做“猜盲盒”，旨在帮助学生学习描述性语言的正确使用。描述性词语常与我们的五种感官相联系：味觉、触觉、视觉、嗅觉和听觉。形容词是最为常见的描述性词语。能正确使用描述性词语，有助于学生口语表达更清晰，写作内容更生动。

游戏中，如果学生触摸后并没有猜出摸到的是什么物件，那么他 / 她可以对该物件进行触感上的描述，比如大小、形状、质地等；如果学生触摸后，已经能够确认物件是什么，那么教师可以鼓励他 / 她对物件进行更进一步的抽象描述，比如其作用和来源等。举个例子，如果学生摸到的是一枚戒指，那么在学生说出 beautiful, glittery 等词语后，教师可以继续引导他 / 她说出 It represents the love between the couple 这样的表达。这样感知、分析、描述物件的过程，也有助于提升学生思维能力。

34 Performer of the Year

Focus: Adverbs of Manner

Level: Intermediate

Duration: 15～20 minutes

Procedure:

- Ask the students to brainstorm the adverbs of manner and write them on the board.
- Divide the class into groups of four. Give each group a set of adverb cards. Ask the students to put them in a pile face down in the middle.
- The students take turns to take a card, think of an action that goes with the adverb on the card and mime the action. Other students in the group guess by asking a question, e.g. "Are you closing the door angrily?" The performer decides whether their guesses are right or wrong by nodding or shaking the head. The first one to guess right wins the card. If nobody can guess right, then the card should be put back on the bottom of the pile. The game continues until there's no card left. The student with the most cards is the winner.

○ 教师要提醒学生，他们不能将所抽卡片上的词直接展示给其他人看，而是要通过表演让其他人猜出来。在表演过程中，他们不能说话或解释，他们只能通过表情或动作来演绎卡片上的方式副词。他们可以在教室范围内随意走动，也可以借助教室内任意物品作为表演道具。

Sample: adverb cards

angrily	anxiously	badly	carefully
cautiously	carelessly	cheerfully	closely
elegantly	enthusiastically	fast	fiercely
gently	happily	hard	heavily
hurriedly	lazily	loudly	nervously
politely	quickly	quietly	rapidly
rudely	sadly	silently	suddenly

这个游戏名为“年度最佳演员”，这是一个表演与猜测的游戏，通过这个游戏可以帮助学生复习方式副词。这个游戏十分考验学生的联想能力和表演能力，当他们看到卡片上的副词时，要立刻联想一个动作将卡片上的副词演绎出来，他们不能用任何口头语言来表达，只能利用自己的面部表情和肢体动作来演绎。这个游戏能很好地解放学生的天性，他们或夸张或滑稽地进行表演，在欢声笑语中，学生不仅能加深对这些方式副词意义的理解，还能更加明确用何动词来与这些方式副词作搭配。

此外，这个表演与猜测的游戏同样适用于情感类形容词的复习，如afraid, angry, happy，等等，学生也可以通过面部表情与动作来演绎和猜测这些形容词。

35 Misprints

Focus: Telling Words (with similar spellings or pronunciations) Apart

Level: Intermediate

Duration: 10～15 minutes

Procedure:

- Divide students into pairs. Prepare each pair a worksheet shown below.
- Raise an example of *whose* and *who's*, and ask students to tell them apart. Let

the students become aware of the confusing words with similar spellings or pronunciations but different meanings in English.

- Ask the students to read through the instructions on the worksheet and try to help Jeremy find and correct the misprints in the extracts from newspapers and magazines.
- Students will be given five minutes to complete the worksheet. By sharing and checking the answer in class, the teacher can encourage students to share their tips on telling the words apart.

○ 在寻找"印刷错误"时，可能会出现找不出错误的情况。教师需仔细观察并倾听学生讨论时的困难点。然后在校对答案时，有意识地邀请某个学生说说他们组遇到的困难，然后鼓励其他小组就该问题分享解决策略。答案校对完毕后，教师也可以就如何区分这些形似、音似的单词展开讨论。

○ 关于完成任务的时间限制，教师可根据学生程度以及任务难度，自行调整。

Examples:

Worksheet

Jeremy has worked as a proofreader for twenty years. His work is to check a newspaper or magazine for correct word choice and spelling before it goes to print. He takes his work seriously and is always considered to be careful enough to find all the errors. However, he has a big eye problem recently. He can't focus on one thing for more than one minute and the doctor suggests he should take a rest. As the deadline is approaching, can you help Jeremy finish his work? Here are the fifteen extracts from newspapers and magazines which all contain a misprint. Please read them carefully, find the wrong word and then suggest which word should have been used instead. You can work with your partner.

	Misprint	**Correct Word**
1. Deaths rise in the dessert as migrants from Mexico try to cross into the U.S. again and again under Biden policy.		
2. She has been working at the Minstry for Defence for seven years, mainly cleaning officers there.		
3. Window, aged 50, good sense of humour, seeks mature man for friendship, possibly marriage.		

续表

Worksheet		
4. Due to the breakdown of the air-conditioning system, rooms will be very hot for the next three days. Please bare with us.		
5. Many people today wear a wrist band that shows their heart rate while people were used to checking their rate by feeling the purse in their wrist or neck.		
6. To clean your oven, put ammonia and water in a pan and sit in the oven.		
7. Politicians are worried about the treat of another war in the Middle East.		
8. President Joe Biden replaces the word 'Mothers', referring to women who both deliver a baby and race a child, with 'Birthing People'.		
9. The winners of the holiday competition will receive free fights, hotel rooms, all meals and 500 dollars.		
10. The ring was too lose on her finger, and Sarah was worried it would slip off.		
11. A storm will bring heavy snow to parts of the southern planes starting Sunday.		
12. Nobel price-winning physicist Steven Weinberg dies at 88.		
13. Heat illnesses: 3 harmful affects of extreme heat on the body		
14. These yummy French cookies are a great snack for the hole family!		
15. Want to lay on a bench chair under the sun with a glass of wine?		

Answers		
	Misprint	Correct word
1.	dessert	desert
2.	officers	offices
3.	window	widow

续表

Answers		
4.	bare	bear
5.	purse	pulse
6.	sit	set
7.	treat	threat
8.	race	raise
9.	fights	flights
10.	lose	loose
11.	planes	plains
12.	price	prize
13.	affects	effects
14.	hole	whole
15.	lay	lie

这个游戏叫做“找找印刷中的错误”，旨在帮助学生区分有着相似发音或拼写的单词。该游戏以 Jeremy 作为刊物校对编辑，却无法完成工作为情境设定，让学生以校对者的身份参与到游戏中。情境及角色的转变，从一定程度上增添了课堂的趣味性，也能为学生参与活动、完成任务带来一种新鲜的体验。游戏环节的设定中，学生需要根据所给信息，找出印刷错误的单词并作修正。游戏中被误用的单词，均是学生在日常学习中容易混淆的。将此类音似、形似的单词以组合的方式呈现，能够引发学生的关注与思考。

在游戏后的互动环节，学生们可以交流彼此区分混淆词的心得，从而使更多的学生在分享中受益。

36 Mind Map

Focus: Associated Words

Level: Intermediate

Duration: 30 minutes

Procedure:

- Tell the class that they are going to see two word lists and they need to try to remember as many words as possible in each round.
- Show the 1st list of words on the screen and give the class 10 seconds to remember them. Pick one learner to recite and see how many words he/she remembers.

  e.g. engine, encyclopedia, headline, soda, department, coin, kangaroo, flower, mechanic, conversation
- Show the 2nd list of words for the class to remember. Once again, pick one learner to recite.

  e.g. daisy, iris, rose, lily, cherry blossom, carnation, tulip, sunflower, jasmine, lotus
- Learners will find it easier to remember the 2nd word list because people are able to remember more words when the words have a connection with each other.
- Tell the class that they are going to learn to make mind maps to link words.
- Draw a circle in the center of the blackboard and write a vocabulary subject there, e.g. car.
- Ask the class to work in groups to brainstorm as many associated words as possible. Then, write the words on the board. See as below:

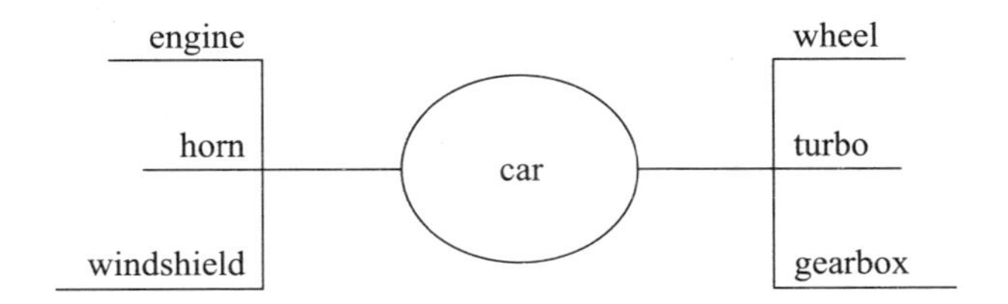

- Give each group some topic cards, a poster and several marker pens. Ask them to choose a topic they're interested in and make a word mind map on the poster.
- Stick the posters on the walls. Ask learners to have a gallery walk and try to remember as many words as possible!

Examples:

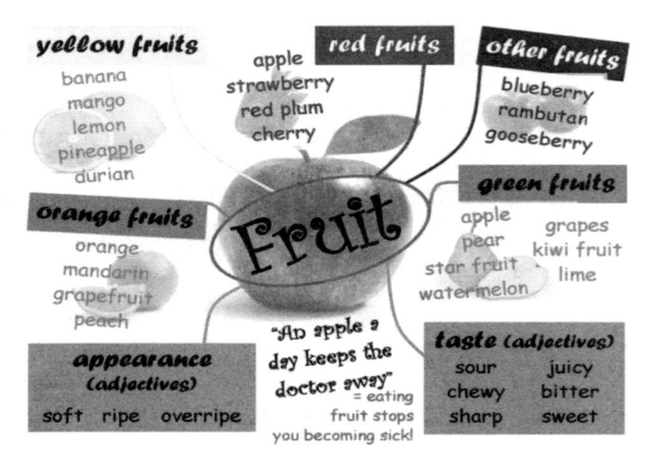

(https://learnenglishteens.britishcouncil.org/sites/teens/files/null/mind_map_for_fruit_v2.jpg)

这个游戏叫做“思维导图”。心理学家认为联想是大脑受到某一刺激时，头脑中出现与该刺激有关的事物形象的心理过程。联想记忆法，就是利用识记对象与客观现实的联系、已知与未知的联系、材料内部各部分之间的联系来记忆的方法，是一种更高效的记忆方法。教师在教词汇的时候可以利用联想帮助学生达到更快记忆的效果，而思维导图则是能实现这一目标的绝佳工具。

思维导图是一种可视化的工具，通过使大脑思维形象化来达到帮助理解和记忆信息的目的。教师通过思维导图能帮助学生建立词与词之间的关联，构建词汇网络，提高词汇学习的效率和自主学习的能力。此外，思维导图也可以用在写作教学中，帮助学生在写作时理清思路；同时，还可以运用在口语教学中，比如，鼓励小组讨论、辩论或演讲时使用思维导图，能有效地帮助学生完成逻辑清晰、有说服力的发言。

37 Build Your Community!

Focus: Community Facilities

Level: Intermediate

Duration: 30 minutes

Procedure:

- Show a video clip of a community. Ask learners to write down the places or facilities appearing in the video.

  Keys: hospital, court, museum, police station, grocery shop, gymnasium.

- Ask learners to think and match the definitions with the public services that corresponds.

- Ask the class to brainstorm more facilities of a community and to tell the services they provide. (Note: Teacher writes down the facilities on the blackboard.)

  e.g. hair salon, restaurant, pharmacy, school, bakery, fire station, park / woodland, cinema, bank, shopping mall, etc.

- Ask the learners to explain the importance of the facilities and how people benefit from them.

  e.g. A 24h pharmacy would be very important in the community because people can get medicine there at convenience. For example, if it's midnight and one child is running a high fever, his/her parents can turn to a 24h pharmacy, a knowledgeable professional is always available there to recommend the medicine to address the child's symptoms.

- Tell the class that the Zoning Commission of Garden Community has posted a notice officially, inviting great ideas and contributions to the town planning.
- Split the class into groups of 4～5. Give each group a large blank poster and a few colored pens. Ask them to design a layout of Garden Community. Draw facilities on the map and write some captions beside the icons, explaining the services the facilities supply.
- Once they complete the design, ask them to stick their posters on the wall of the classroom. Each group chooses one member to stand beside the poster and introduce their design.
- The other groups members walk around in the classroom. Listen to the introduction of other groups. They can also talk with the presenters to get more information.
- Learners can stick a star on the design they like. The group gets the most stars wins the Best Designer!

该游戏名为"建设社区"。近些年，Community（社区）的概念在国内被日益强化，城市学生基本理解社区的概念、熟练掌握社区功能服务的相关表达，是十分必要的。

本例活动旨在帮助学生学习和巩固社区配套设施的表达方式，通过观看视频以及图文配对的方法，帮助学生初步了解社区常见服务设施的名称；通过头脑风暴进一步引出词汇、丰富素材，为后面两个环节做好铺垫；通过小组设计 Garden Community 的蓝图，使学生对社区设施进一步理解；最后环节展示、解说设计图，投票选出最佳设计，能激发学生的热情和参与，巩固学生对社区配套设施的理解。

38 You Can't Tell!

Focus: Phrasal Verb

Level: Advanced

Duration: 30 minutes

Procedure:

- Prepare some cards with phrasal verbs. Show a series of slides of phrasal verbs and pictures. Ask learners to guess what the phrasal verbs mean with the help of pictures.

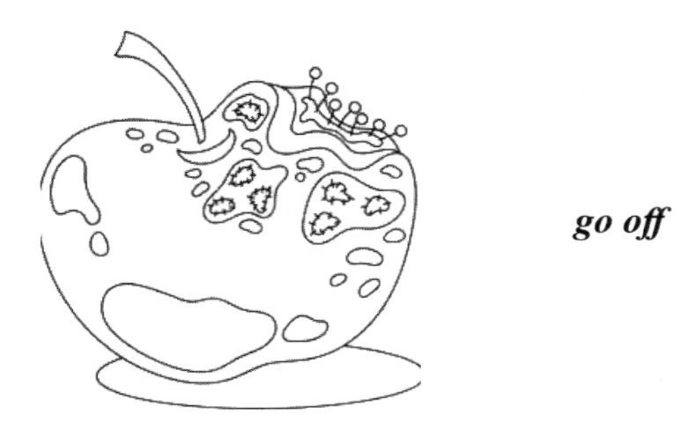

go off

e.g. If food goes off, it becomes too bad to eat.

- Split the class into different groups of 4～6. Send out cards to each group. The cards should be put face down to the table.
- Players take turns to get a card and stick the cards on their foreheads. (Note: They can only see others' cards but cannot see their own.)
- Players start a free conversation clockwise. Each player tries to induce other players to speak out the words on their cards. At the same time, each player needs to think what words they get and tries to avoid saying it. (Rule: If the player mentions the word on his/her own card, he/she loses in that round. He/she needs to pick another card and the game continues...)
- After all the cards have been used, the game ends. The one who has least cards wins!

Examples:

Player	Cards he/she gets
P1	listen to the music
P2	look after
P3	hang out
P4	back up

Here's the conversation:

Player 1: How would you like to spend your weekend?

Player 2: I usually read books at home.

Player 3: Oh, I'd like to hang out with my friends.

Player 3 said the forbidden words, so he/she loses in this round. He/she keeps the card and picks a new one. The game continues.

这个游戏名为“心口难辨”，该游戏旨在帮助学生训练短语动词的使用。短语动词是词汇中的重要组成部分，也是同学们学习过程中的难点之一。它存在一定挑战性，往往是基于以下两点原因。

一是短语动词由两个单词构成，组合后的含义却往往与原词含义不同，给学生造成了一定困扰。比如，*hang out* 中 *hang* 解释为“悬挂”，*out* 解释为“外”，但组合后的 *hang out* 却解释为“闲逛”。

二是有些短语动词在不同的语境中也存在不同的含义。比如，*pass out* 在句子“*If he took one more drink, he would pass out.*”中该词解释为“晕倒，失去知觉”，但在句子“*The teacher hasn't finished passing out the tests yet.*”中则解释为“分发”。

虽然短语动词的学习有难度，但它们在日常生活中使用频率很高，因此很重要，教师可以使用以上游戏，帮助学生巩固短语动词，熟练运用短语动词。

39 Jobs Wanted

Focus: Consolidating the Vocabulary About Jobs and Personalities

Level: Advanced

Duration: 30～45 minutes

Procedure:

- Divide students into groups of 4～5. Students take turns to read out their job riddles of four lines (which they've prepared in advance) and ask their group members to guess what they are.

- Ask students to have a group discussion and finish the exercise by judging what the characters are like according to their descriptions about themselves. Then the teacher checks the answer orally.

○ 游戏一和游戏二，其目的在于帮助学生复习关于工作和人物性格的两类词汇。提前扫除词汇障碍可以为接下来的招聘广告游戏做好铺垫。如果学生程度较好，教师可以省略这两个环节。

- Ask students to read the poster and help Disneyland Park make a detailed job advertisement as requested.
- Ask groups to present their advertisements to the whole class and explain their design.

Examples:

Game one: Job riddles	
1. I move people around. I almost sit all day. I drive a car. I charge a fare. (a taxi driver)	2. I work in the sky. I'm often a woman. I serve food and drinks. I'm usually good-looking. (a flight attendant)
3. I work with scissors. I work in a salon. I wash, dry and brush. I make people look better. (a hairdresser)	4. I wear a uniform. I often carry a gun. I catch thieves. I help people solve problems. (a policeman)

○ 在设计谜语前，教师可以提醒学生从以下几个方面来设计谜面：1. Where does he/she work? 2. What does he/she usually do? 3. What does he/she need to wear at work? 4. What does he/she need to take? 5. What do people think of this job? 此外，教师需向学生强调，谜面的设定要指向明确，但又不能太过直白。教师可通过举例加以说明。

该游戏改编自：https://server4.liveworksheets.com/worksheets/en/English_as_a_Second_Language_(ESL)/Vocabulary/Game*_Job_Riddles_pe628850gi

Game Two: Describing character

Describing character

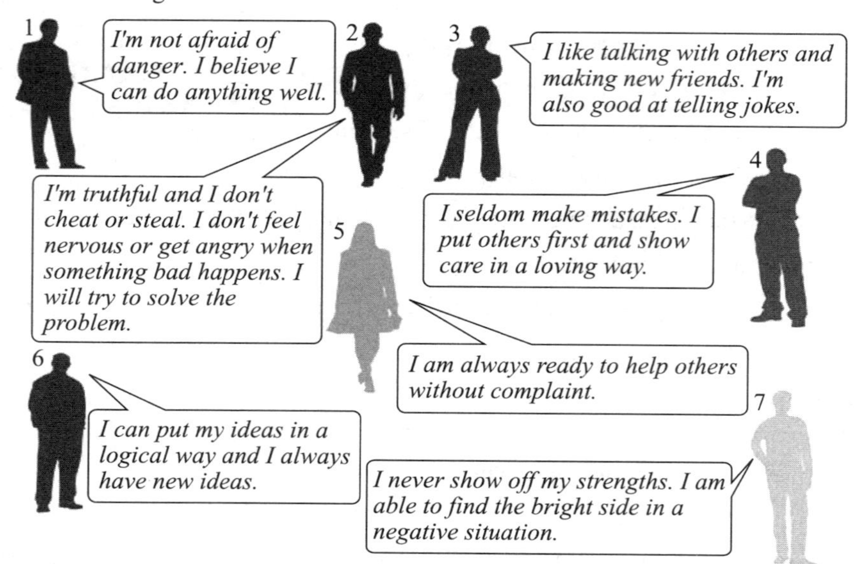

Complete the sentences with the appropriate adjectives.

1. Billyis a b__________ and c__________ person.
2. Robert is an h__________ and c__________ person.
3. Amy is a s__________ and h__________ person.
4. Jack is a c__________ and t__________ person.
5. Kate is a k__________ and p__________ person.
6. Paul is a w__________ and c__________ person.
7. George is a h__________ and p__________ person.

Possible answers:

1. brave; confident
2. honest; calm
3. sociable; humorous
4. careful; thoughtful
5. kind; patient
6. well-organized; creative
7. humble; positive

○ 该环节中，为降低难度，教师可以将形容词的首字母提供给学生。如果学生程度较好，可以去除首字母的限制，但同时，教师也需要明白标准答案并非唯一。

该游戏改编自：https://en.islcollective.com/preview/201311/b1/describing-character-part-2_61760_1.jpg

Game Three: Making a job advertisement

Work in groups and read the poster below. Choose one job and make a detailed job advertisement accordingly. You need to include the following information in your advertisement like position, job description, preferences and applications to and etc.

○ 在制作招聘广告时需要囊括空缺职位、职位描述、职位倾向（也就是希望应聘者具备什么样的性格或能力）以及如何应聘等信息；并且在小组分享环节说出制定该标准的理由。教师也可以根据每组招聘广告上的信息，进行提问。同时，为了使广告呈现出更佳的视觉效果，教师可以事先为每一组准备彩笔和海报纸。

这个游戏叫做“职位空缺”，旨在帮助学生巩固关于工作及人物性格两类词汇的基础上，进一步思考不同工作岗位与不同性格的匹配度，从而提升学生思维品质。三个小游戏由浅入深，层层递进。尤其是最后一个设计招聘广告的游戏，不仅仅是基于词汇的训练，更需要学生过渡到短语以及句子的完整表达。最后的交流环节则考查了学生是否能清晰地表达广告设计的理由。这样循序渐进的游戏环节不仅促进了相关英语词汇的学习和使用，而且能够使学生对于不同职业要求及发展有一个更清晰的认知。

40 Vocabulary Auction

Focus: Word Meaning

Level: All levels

Duration: 30 minutes

Procedure:

- Get prepared a list of words your learners have been studying, some chips and a mallet.
- Split the class into groups of 3～4. Give each group some chips of $1000.

(Note: Teacher needs to prepare your own supply, to pay out groups who double down later in the game.)

- Teacher acts as an auctioneer, showing one word on the screen each time and then players bid for it. To make the game funnier, teacher can say "Going once, going twice, SOLD!" , like a real auctioneer. Of course, the word goes to the highest bidder.
- Now that the auction is over, it's time for players to try to win their money back. Teacher shows the word list once again and have the winning group define the word.
- If the winning group can define the word correctly, they get the chips back. Plus, they can double down by using the word correctly in a sentence.
- If the winning group fail to define the word, the second highest bidder gets a chance. If they are also unsuccessful, the next highest bidder gets a chance, and so on, until one group gets it right.
- The game continues until all the words are defined. The group with the most chips win.

○ 学生定义单词的方式，除直接用英文释义外，也可以通过近义词、举例子等方式。只要能证明学生已理解该单词，就判定正确。

Examples:

For the word *nation*, bidders can win their money back as long as they manage to give a(n):

(1) definition: a country, considered especially in relation to its people and its social or economic structure.

(2) synonym: country.

(3) example: China is one of the greatest nations in the world.

这个游戏叫做“单词竞拍”，模拟了真实的拍卖会场景。游戏分为“竞拍单词”和“释义回本”两个主要环节，不仅能让学生在竞争与挑战中高效地复习巩固了单词，也为他们提供了良好的听说环境。

其实，竞拍的创意不仅可以用在词汇教学中，词法、语法的学习也可以借用这一手段。比如，教师可以把拍卖的对象变成拍卖情态动词 can, must, may, should 等，学生竞拍后，要求他们用拍得的情态动词给出一个合理的语境，或者还原一个合理的对话，以此来考查他们是不是能正确地使用情态动词。当然，内容还可以变成考查时态、句型等。总之，游戏只是一个框架，教师可以灵活地替换练习内容。

Part Three

Grammar
（语法）

41 Snap

Focus: Time Prepositions

Level: Elementary

Duration: 15～20 minutes

Procedure:

- Divide the students into pairs. Give each pair two sets of cards. The cards are prepared in advance with different time prepositions (at, in, on...) written on one set while different time phrases on the other. Both students randomly take one set. They shuffle the cards and place the pile face down in front of them.

○ 由于该游戏考察的是学生短时间内迅速做出反应的能力，因此教师需要着重强调：在游戏开始前，卡片务必背面朝上；游戏开始后，同组对抗的两位学生需在同一时间翻卡片，以确保比赛的公平公正。

- When the game starts, both students turn over a card from the top of their pile at the same time. If the time preposition matches with the time phrase, the first student to say “Snap” can take back his card and place it face down at the bottom of his pile. If he/she wants to win the opponent’s card, he/she should make a true sentence by using the time preposition and phrase. If the sentence is grammatically and logically correct, the student gets the opponent’s card and puts it aside. If the time preposition and time phrase don’t match, the students continue turning over cards until a matching pair comes up and someone says “Snap” . If a student says “Snap” when the cards don’t match, the other student wins the two cards and the game continues. If two students shout out “snap” at the same time and the two cards do match, both of the students should take back the card and turn over the next one. The one who manages to collect five cards from his/her opponent wins the game. Then the

○ 如果比赛双方不能对句子的正误判定达成一致，可以现场请求教师协助。

○ 游戏中，累计获得对手5张卡片为最终的获胜者。一轮游戏结束后，教师可以根据课堂安排、学生表现等因素，考虑是否进行第二轮。若展开第二轮对决，可以要求两位学生手持与第一轮不同的另一组卡片。

two students can sort the cards into two sets and start another round with a different set.

Examples:

Time prepositions			
in	in	in	in
at	at	at	at
on	on	on	on
during	during	for	for
no preposition	no preposition	no preposition	no preposition

Time phrases			
autumn	Friday	the 1st of August	night
Christmas	this afternoon	3 o'clock	the morning
last week	New Year's Eve	the 20th century	every weekend
an hour	tomorrow	a few days	a minute
next Wednesday	my birthday	2020	the winter vacation

这个游戏叫做“配对儿”，旨在帮助学生进一步巩固时间短语与介词的搭配。游戏中，学生需要始终保持注意力的集中，关注每一次双方卡片上的内容是否配对成功，以“先声夺人”喊出“Snap”的方式，抢占比赛得分的先机。为获取对方卡片，学生还需要在成功配对介词和时间短语后，用该时间状语造句。遣词造句不仅考察学生对于时态的正确判别，也考验了学生的语言素养以及对语言情境的理解。另外值得一提的是，有些时间短语前不需要加介词，譬如上述样例中的 *last week*，*next Wednesday*，*tomorrow*，*every weekend*，*this afternoon*，在用作时间状语时，无需介词。将此类易混淆的短语一并囊括于游戏中，其目的是希望学生能够关注差异，辨析不同，从而进一步理解和强化这些规则。此外，教师还可以使用该游戏来巩固介词和地点状语的搭配，只需将卡片上的内容稍作修改即可。

42 Tic-Tac-Toe

Focus: Using Possessive Pronouns

Level: Elementary

Duration: 15 minutes

- Split the class into small groups. Give each group a game board, a dice, counters and a pen.
- Players take turns to roll the dice. Each number represents different possessive pronouns. Look at the chart to find which possessive pronouns you must use for that roll.

  e.g. 1=mine, 2=yours, 3=hers, 4=his, 5=ours, 6=theirs
- Find a sentence which requires that possessive pronoun.
- Cover that square with one of your counters if your answer is correct. (If there are no squares available, your turn is over.)
- The first player to cover a line of 3 squares (vertically, horizontally or diagonally) with his/her counters wins the game.

Examples:

If you want a slice. Ask Tamia because the pizza is ______.	Tina's book is on her desk. That book is ______.	Michael wrote the book report, so it is ______.
I own that scooter. That scooter is ______.	The present was given to Dan and Frank. The present is ______.	The red jacket belongs to you. The jacket is ______.
I found a lucky penny, so it is ______ to keep.	My cousins and I bought that bucket, so it is ______.	Abigail bought the blue pen, so it is ______.

Keys: hers, hers, his, mine, theirs, yours, mine, ours, hers

Mr. Franks gave him that sticker, so it is ______.	Harry bought that skateboard, so it is ______.	You and Ella earned this money. This money is ______.
My sister and I own a tent. The tent is ______.	This sandwich was in your lunchbox, so it is ______.	My eraser is smaller than your eraser. The smaller eraser is ______.
Lucy purchased the hat, so it is ______.	This baseball belongs to Jack and Lisa. The baseball is ______.	Those kittens belong to Mr. Tucker. They are ______.

Keys: his, his, yours, ours, yours, mine, hers, theirs, his

Your parents' car is outside. That car is ______.	Leah and I own that bicycle. That bicycle is ______.	I got you this present, so it is ______ to open.
The mailman brought their mail. The mail is ______.	My parents and I live in that house. That house is ______.	I earned that homework pass, so it is ______ to use.
If you want the last cookie, it is ______.	My tower is taller than Jamie's. The shorter tower is ______.	The game belongs to you and Eric. The game is ______.

Keys: theirs, ours, yours, theirs, ours, mine, yours, hers, yours

该游戏名叫“三连棋”，旨在帮助学生巩固名词性物主代词的使用。英语中的物主代词分为形容词性物主代词与名词性物主代词，学生常常将两者混淆起来，因此这是基础语法教学中的一个难点。这个游戏可以让学生在趣味练习中巩固语法知识。

43 Sense the Pictures!

Focus: Sensory Verbs

Level: Elementary

Duration: 10～15 minutes

Procedure:

- Divide the students into pairs (student A and B). Prepare each pair a set of pictures and two number boards.
- The students put the pictures face up in front of them and have two minutes to take a look at the pictures. Then student A chooses six pictures secretly and describes the pictures one by one in terms of how they look, taste, smell, sound or feel. Then student B needs to find the matching pictures and place them over the squares from one to six. While describing the pictures, student A is required to use sensory verbs only and for each turn. Student A has to use at least two different sensory verbs in his/her description. If student B is not sure and wants to get more information, he/she can further raise questions. For example, "*What does it look/taste/smell/sound/feel like?*" After student B finishes his board, student A reveals the answer. Then the pair can swap roles and repeat the game.

○ 游戏开始前，教师可以给学生两分钟的时间熟悉图片的内容，以便学生在之后的环节中可以快速地确定要描述的图片。教师需强调，仅能使用感官动词进行描述。为确保提示指向明确，描述方每次必须使用至少两个不同的感官动词。如若另一方根据线索无法确定哪一幅图片，描述方需进一步从其他角度对图片进行补充描述。

○ 为了游戏能够顺利进行，教师可以在游戏开始前，引导学生以头脑风暴的方式归纳整理出不同感官体验对应的形容词，以便学生在游戏中能够自如地表达。

Examples:

The Number Board		
1	2	3
4	5	6

这个游戏叫做“我说你找”，旨在帮助学生通过描述图片来进一步复习感官动词后接形容词的用法。学生需要通过五官的感受来描述图片中的事物，而另一方则需确定所描述的图片是哪一幅并移动图片至指定区域。教师在准备图片时，可以有意识地加入一些外观、口味、触感相似的事物，以增加描述的难度，从而促使学生尽可能多地使用不同的感官动词进行多角度的描述。例如在上述样例中，a pencil，a cigarette end 以及 a knife，就其外观而言，学生均可以用“It looks straight.”来进行描述，此时，就需要学生进一步提供指向明确的信息来帮助猜图一方，如补充“It smells terrible, but some people love it.”的细节描述，猜图方就能快速作出判断，确定描述的是 a cigarette end。整个游戏过程中，教师需从旁协助，解决学生表述中的生词障碍。游戏结束后，教师还可以要求学生选出一两幅最难描述的图片，通过集体讨论来帮助学生打开思路。

44 Chain Stories

Focus: Regular and Irregular Past Forms

Level: Lower-intermediate and above

Duration: 15～20 minutes

Procedure:

- Prepare cards with the simple form of different verbs in advance.
- Divide the students into groups of 5～6. Give each student a card and provide each group with a sentence to begin their story.
- Ask students go around in their circle and add a sentence to their story by using the verb given.
- Invite groups to repeat their stories to the class. The whole class may vote for the best one according to the checklist.

○ 在学生开始编故事之前，教师可以提醒学生，在叙述一个故事的时候，我们通常用一般过去时。另外，教师还需引导学生关注所编故事内容，可以是严肃的，也可以是滑稽的，但不管哪一种，都要合乎情理、言之有物。

Examples:

The starting sentence:	That was an unlucky day.
The verbs given:	break; miss; try; feel; forget; have
Student A:	On my way to the campus, my father's car broke down.
Student B:	Because of it, I missed an important lecture.
Student C:	I tried to explain my lateness but my professor thought it was just an excuse.
Student D:	I felt really upset and decided to go back home by underground.
Student E:	However, when I reached the station, I found I forgot to wear a mask.
Student F:	Unfortunately, I had no choice but to walk back home.

○ 续说故事的目的在于帮助学生巩固一般过去时动词变形规则，但如果学生语言功底较好，在续说故事中使用了其他符合故事逻辑的时态，如过去进行时、过去完成时、过去将来时等，教师还是应当予以鼓励及肯定。

Checklist	
1. Does the story cover all the verbs required?	☆☆☆☆☆☆
2. Are the verbs used correctly?	☆☆☆☆☆☆
3. Are the sentences coherently and logically linked with each other?	☆☆☆☆☆☆
4. If the story is funny or special, you can give bonus stars.	☆☆☆☆☆☆

这个游戏叫做“故事接龙”，旨在通过共同编故事的方式来帮助学生复

习一般过去时中动词的变形规则。这个游戏的乐趣在于每一位学生都可以为故事贡献自己的创意，从而促使学生主动思考。同时，小组投票的环节在一定程度上也会激发学生的兴趣，提升参与度。学生投票的依据应该满足检查清单上的内容，比如是否正确使用动词过去式，故事是否符合逻辑，故事是否具有趣味性等。

根据学生的学习水平，教师还可以适当提高游戏难度。譬如，要求学生丰富句式的种类，续写的语句可以从单一的肯定句拓宽到否定句、疑问句、感叹句，也可以从简单句上升到并列句、复合句等。这个活动也适用于其他时态动词变形的操练。教师可以根据教学需求进行改动。

45 The Quarantine Hotel

Focus: Modal Verbs

Level: Intermediate

Duration: 15～20 minutes

Procedure:

- Divide the students into groups of 5～6. Provide each group with a copy of the worksheet shown below.
- Tell the students that they will have to manage one of the quarantine hotels in Shanghai. They are required to discuss in groups and come up with rules for guests, staff and hotel by using different modal verbs, such as *should/shouldn't, must/mustn't, can/can't, need, have to, etc.*
- After all the groups finish writing, each group should appoint a representative. The representative of each group will share their "hotel regulations", while the other groups need to listen and take notes.
- Any reasonable and grammatically correct regulation will be awarded with one point. Meanwhile, any group who helps to correct the grammar mistake or gives advice on revision wins one point, too. The game goes on until the last group finishes. The 10 bonus

○ 为了鼓励学生在讨论规则时尽可能使用不同的情态动词，教师可以对在规则中使用最多不同情态动词的小组进行加分的奖励。

points will be given to the group which covers the most modal verbs of different types. In the end, the group with the highest scores wins the game.

Examples:

In order to prevent the spread of COVID-19, those entering Shanghai from abroad are required to quarantine in the designated hotel for 14 days. Suppose you have just taken over the management of one of these hotels. Discuss in groups and decide what rules you are going to have for guests, staff and hotel. Try to use varied modal verbs to describe the rules.

Guests	Rules
(Rooms, Meals, Health check...)	1. 2. 3. ...
Staff	**Rules**
(Working hours, Work assignment, Self-protection...)	1. 2. 3. ...
Hotel	**Rules**
(Facilities, Area arrangement,...)	1. 2. 3. ...

○ 为了帮助学生打开思维，教师可以在学习单中适当给予提示。

Possible answers:

(1) Guests can open the window for fresh air in their rooms and order grocery delivery if necessary.

(2) Guests must take a temperature check three times a day on their own and send in the result by Wechat.

(3) Guests have to pack and seal their own rubbish and put it outside their room at 8 o'clock every morning.

(4) All the staff must be fully masked and suited.

(5) Staff should serve the meals on time.

(6) Staff have to disinfect the corridors every 4 hours.

(7) The hotel ought not to accept non-quarantine guests.

(8) The hotel is supposed to be equipped with several doctors.

(9) The hotel needs to arrange certain clean and safe areas for staff to take a rest.

(10) ...

这个游戏叫做“隔离酒店”，旨在帮助学生进一步理解和巩固不同情态动词的含义和使用情境。该游戏以疫情时代为背景，要求学生以酒店管理者的视角来思考防疫守则。这不仅考察了学生生活知识的贮备，也考验了其作为领导者多角度思考问题的能力。因此，相比“纸上谈兵”的语法训练，不妨试着为学生创设一个合理的情境，将语法点的操练巧妙地融入其中，让学生在不知不觉中强化这些规则的使用。

游戏结束后，教师还可以要求学生通过倾听其他组的想法，进一步对规则做修改和补充，并制作成海报张贴于教室内。这样做可以激发学生的再次交流，同时该话题核心词汇的反复呈现也有助于学生加深记忆。

46 Roll the Dice

Focus: Phrasal Verbs

Level: All levels

Duration: 20～25 minutes

Procedure:

- Before the game, divide the students into groups of 3～4. Prepare each group a game board, a set of cards, counters and a dice. On the front side of each card is the verb that gives a hint such as *GET, TAKE, PUT, TURN, LOOK, etc.* while on the opposite side is a sentence that needs to be paraphrased. The cards with the same verb are placed in the same pile on the table, and all the cards should be shuffled.

GET front side	*I **left the bus** at the wrong station so I had to wait for another one.* opposite side

- During the game, all the players take turns to roll the dice and move their counters along the board. When a player lands on a square with a verb, such as "GET", the player next to him/her picks up a card from the top of the "GET" pile and reads aloud the sentence. The player listens to the sentence and then needs to use a suitable phrasal verb with "GET" to rephrase the sentence and change the form of the phrasal verb as requested. If the player could paraphrase the sentence both correctly and completely, he/she moves forward one space and keeps the card. If not, he/she misses a turn and the card needs to be placed at the bottom of the pile. The first person to get to the FINISH sign wins the game.

○ 教师可以采取两种方式来检验学生是否替换正确。一是直接将答案写在句子的后面，由读题学生来进行判定。二是教师不提供正确答案，由同组其他玩家来判定正误。

Examples:

Game Board

1 START	2 GET	3 PUT	4 *Miss a turn*	5 TURN	6 GO
12 LOOK	11 *Go forward to 15*	10 GET	9 GO	8 THINK	7 *Go back to 4*
13 TURN	14 GO	15	16 TAKE	17 *Miss a turn*	18 TURN
24 *Change your position with one of the other players*	23 TAKE	22 LOOK	21 PUT	20 BREAK	19 GO
25 PUT	26 GET	27 SET	28 *Miss a turn*	29 TAKE	30 *Go back to 15*
36 *Miss a turn*	35 *Go forward to 38*	34 GO	33 TURN	32 *Start again!*	31 THINK
37 TAKE	38	39 *Change your position with one of the other players*	40 SET	41 PUT	42 TAKE
48 FINISH	47 THINK	46 LOOK	45 BREAK	44 *Go back to 38*	43 TURN

The sentences written on the cards

GET	(1) I left the bus at the wrong station so I had to wait for another one. (got off) (2) Because of staying up late, I didn't get out of my bed until noon the next day.(get up) (3) I have a good relationship with all my classmates. (get on/along well with) (4) When Linda tried to contact me, I had already arrived at the airport. (got to)
TAKE	(1) The plane couldn't leave the ground and fly because of a storm. (take off) (2) With increasing cases of COVID-19, please don't remove your mask in the public places. (take off) (3) This desk fills too much room. Can we replace it with a smaller one? (takes up) (4) In his seventies, Tom began to develop an interest in gardening. (took up) (5) I'm eager to get out of the city and breathe some mountain air. (take in) (6) I listened carefully and took notes in class, but I haven't comprehended everything.(taken in)
...	...

○ 教师在出题时，需注意同一词组不同含义的辨析（如 TAKE 中 第 3、5 句）。可重复考察学生对同一词组的掌握情况，但句子的情境需不同（如 TAKE 中第 3、4 句）。每一组需准备多少张卡片，由同组玩游戏的人数和该动词在游戏中出现的次数决定。例如：参与游戏的人数为 3 人，“SET”在游戏盘中共出现 2 次，则对应“SET”组别的卡片需准备 6 张以上。

这个游戏叫做“掷骰子”，旨在帮助学生区分动词搭配不同介词的词义差别。该游戏模仿飞行棋的游戏规则，使学生根据掷骰点数和改句任务，完成前进或后退。棋盘中还囊括了暂停一轮、与对手交换位置等趣味性设置，以此提升游戏中的未知感、刺激感。

玩游戏前，教师可以根据学情筛选出学生容易混淆的动词词组，并要求学生自查后，对没有掌握的词义进行造句。待教师检查后，将词组用同义词替换后誊写于卡片上。这样做一来可以减轻教师准备大量词句的负担，二来可以基于学生的共性问题开展更具针对性的操练。上述样例中囊括的 9 个动词，放在一起来检测，难度较大，教师可以根据实际情况做删减。

在游戏结束后，教师还可以要求学生以小组为单位，继续对剩余卡片上的句子进行同义句替换。可以要求学习程度较好的同学（也就是手上卡片较多的同学）来启发帮助能力较弱的同学，使人人参与其中，收获其中。

47 Anti-quiz

Focus: Superlative Forms of Adjectives and Adverbs

Level: Lower-intermediate

Duration: 15～20 minutes

Procedure:

- Divide the students into groups of 4～5. Each group must prepare six answers and their matching questions to ask other groups.
- After four or five minutes' preparation, each group chooses four answers and takes turns to read out the answers one by one. The first group to correctly articulate the question and spell the superlative form of adjective or adverb gets one point. If no group can figure out the "question", the group who comes up with the "answer" gets one point instead. No repetition is allowed.
- When all the "answers" have been "questioned", the group with the most points is declared the winner.

○ 在准备阶段，教师要求每组学生想出6个答案及相对应的问题，而在比赛环节，只需选出其中4个对其他小组进行发问，这样做是为了避免问题重复，多想出两个以备用。此外，教师应当巡视每一组的准备情况，确保问题和答案的准确性。

Examples:

Answers:	**Questions:**
Ben	Who runs (the) fastest/ most quickly in our class?
Blue whale	What is the existing heaviest animal?
February	Which month has the least days?
Hainan	What is the second biggest island in China?
China	Which country has the largest population in Asia?
Astronaut Jing Haipeng	Which astronaut has been to the space the most times in China?

这个游戏叫做“反测验”。不同于教师抛出问题，学生进行回答的单向模式，在“反测验”中，教师将两项任务颠倒过来，让学生反过来根据答案思考问题是什么，形成教师与学生、学生与学生间的双向互动模式。该游戏旨在激发学生学习兴趣，帮助其巩固形容词及副词最高级的变形规则。该游戏不仅能帮助学生巩固知识点，同时也能锻炼学生遣词造句的能力。

值得一提的是，由于学生在比赛中需要思考最……的人或事或物，因此，教师可以引导学生在思考问题时不要仅局限于所见之处，可以拓宽至社会乃至国家层面，譬如中国之最、世界之最等。学生在打破思维局限时，不同学科的知识在教学中得以渗透，在无形中实现学生综合运用能力的提高。

48 Shout It Out!

Focus: Contrasting Adjectives and Adverbs

Level: Intermediate

Duration: 10～15 minutes

Procedure:

- Write the adjectives which will be used later on the blackboard.
- Divide the students into groups of 3～4 and ask each group to select a spokesperson.
- Teacher read the sample text aloud and pause where marked. Groups should quickly choose the right word and change it into an adverb if necessary. The spokesperson then should shout it out and spell it correctly if the form is changed. The first group to provide the correct answer gets one point. If the pause occurs at a place where no adverb or adjective would be possible, the spokesperson should shout “zero”.
- The team which gains the most points will be given the title of “*Quick Minds*”.

○ 为增加游戏难度，可适当增加几个易混淆的形容词。

○ 注意：每个词仅能使用一次。

○ 积分规则：如果正确答案没有发生变形，只需喊出这个词即可；如果存在变形，不仅需要喊出该词，还需拼读正确；如果不需要填词，则需要喊出 zero；完成以上要求，方可获得加分。

Examples:

<table>
<tr><td>The adjectives given:
gentle, fierce, soon, hard, short, fast, total, lucky, friendly, dark, cold, warm, comfortable, big, small</td></tr>
<tr><td>Sample text:
It was Friday morning. The wind was blowing (pause) and the sky was getting (pause). “Hurry up, dear. It’s going to rain (pause).” said Mum. So I packed my bag as (pause) as possible and rushed out of my room (pause). However, (pause) after I ran out of my house, it began to pour with rain. I got (pause) wet even with a (pause) umbrella in my hand. I tried (pause) to find somewhere to hide, but I failed. (pause), I saw a café in the end. The café owner was so (pause) that she invited me to stay inside and offered me a towel and a cup of hot water. I felt (pause) and (pause).</td></tr>
<tr><td>Completed text:
It was Friday morning. The wind was blowing <u>fiercely</u> and the sky was getting <u>dark</u>. “Hurry up, dear. It’s going to rain <u>soon</u>.” said Mum. So I packed my bag as <u>fast</u> as possible and rushed out of my room <u>(zero)</u>. However, <u>shortly</u> after I ran out of my house, it began to pour with rain. I got <u>totally</u> wet even with a <u>big</u> umbrella in my hand. I tried <u>hard</u> to find somewhere to hide, but I failed. <u>Luckily</u>, I saw a café in the end. The café owner was so <u>friendly</u> that she invited me to stay inside and offered me a towel and a cup of hot water. I felt <u>warm</u> and <u>comfortable</u>.</td></tr>
</table>

这个游戏叫做“大声喊出来”，旨在进一步巩固学生在连贯语境中，对形容词和副词用法的区分。有别于常规的阅读填词，该活动以小组为单位，采用听说的方式对学生进行语言知识和语言能力的考察。这个活动的挑战在于学生需根据教师所念的文本，在停顿处，挑选合适的词进行文本补充。这考验了学生获取信息的能力及临场反应能力。同时，“以赛促学”的形式，也能激发学生团队协作能力。

在游戏结束后，教师可以要求学生齐声朗读短文，并由学生归纳总结形容词和副词的变形规则，以达到对知识点的巩固效果。此外，教师还可以根据学生水平，适当调整任务难度。譬如，将目标词的变形要求改为形容词、副词的比较级和最高级，或进一步延伸至名词、动词互相之间的转换等。

49 Vocabulary Clock

Focus: Telling the Time and Reviewing the Words

Level: Elementary and lower-intermediate

Duration: 10～15 minutes

Procedure:

- Give students a vocabulary list and ask them to go over the words in advance.
- Draw a vocabulary clock on the blackboard (like the example shown below).

○ 教师在准备词汇列表时，可以有意识地加入近期所学的一些重、难点词，从而促使学生主动地去记、去背。

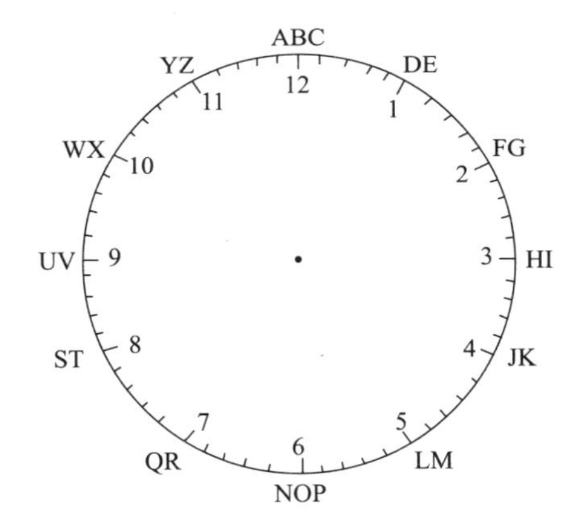

- Divide students into groups of the same size.
- Teacher randomly choose a word from the list and call it out. When students hear the word, they have to figure out with which letter the word starts and with which letter it ends. Then they need to find the corresponding numbers to which the two letters point. As the first letter of the word refers to the hour hand while the last letter refers to the minute hand, the students can then get the time. Raise the word "seize" as an example. According to the rules

○ 具体的积分规则如下：如果学生使用从左到右的时间表达方式，加 1 分；如果是从右到左借助介词的表达方式，则加 2 分；如若两种方式都使用，并且表达都正确，则加 3 分。

mentioned above, the first letter of the word is "s" which refers to "8" on the clock while the last letter "e" refers to "1" on the clock. With the hour hand pointing to "8" and minute hand pointing to "1" , the time is "eight five" or "five past eight" . The first student who tells the time correctly scores one to three points, depending on which way he/she uses. The group with the highest score wins the game. During the game, the teacher needs to encourage all the students to participate.

这个游戏叫做"词汇钟"，旨在帮助学生巩固时间的表达。该游戏的新颖之处在于它把报时和词汇学习融汇在一起。学生想要知道准确的时间，就必须对词汇表里单词的读音和拼写了然于胸。游戏中的"眼耳并用"能让学生具有更强的感知识别能力，学生表面上只玩了一个游戏，但事实上却达到了玩两个游戏的效果，可谓一举两得。

在上述样例中，数字钟里的字母是按照字母表顺序排列的。为了增加游戏的难度，教师可以把这些字母打乱。此外，这个游戏也可以反着玩，教师说出时间，学生识别出对应的首尾字母，以此推断出所学的某个词汇，进行拼读巩固。

50 Dominoes

Focus: Gerunds and Infinitives

Level: Intermediate

Duration: 15~20 minutes

Procedure:

- Divide students into groups of 3. Prepare each group two sets of dominoes (A and B). Write different verbs such as *avoid, hate, decide, would like* on the set A while gerunds and infinitives on the set B.

○ 教师在准备两组多米诺骨牌时，请务必在卡片的背面标记字母 A/B 加以区分，以防学生混淆。

- Ask the students to separately shuffle the two sets of dominoes, and place them in two piles face down. Then deal out five A dominoes for each player.

- Tell the students to turn over the top domino from the pile B and put it on the table. Then the first player needs to use one of the dominoes in his/her hand to match with the domino on the table, making a correct verb-gerund or verb-infinitive collocation. Additionally, he/she needs to make a sentence by using the well-matched phrase. If the sentence is logically and grammatically correct, the player could leave the domino that he/she has just put down on the table permanently. If not, the player has to take the domino back again.The same rule goes for the one who isn't able to make a sentence with the well-matched phrase.

○ 在配对两张多米诺骨牌时，学生必须考虑结构和含义是否同时匹配。譬如：桌上的卡片是 swimming，而学生手中的卡片是 finish, practise, decide, fail, plan，就结构而言，finish 和 practise 均满足后接动名词的要求，但 finish swimming 的这种表达略显突兀，因此，学生在配对时还应思考词义的匹配性。

- The other players then take turns to match their dominoes in the same way. If a player can't put down one of his dominoes, round one comes to an end and he/she has to take one domino from the top of the pile A as "punishment" . Meanwhile, he/she is given the chance to start a new round by turning over the top domino from the pile B again. If there are no dominoes left in the pile A, the player needs to play passes to the next player. The first one to get rid of all the dominoes in his/her hand wins the game.

○ 如果在几轮游戏后，A 组牌被拿光，那么无法成功配对的玩家只能将出牌权让给下一位玩家。

Examples:

Dominoes (set A)				
like	hate	forget	remember	stop
continue	try	suggest	enjoy	mind
avoid	practise	consider	keep	imagine
admit	deny	finish	decide	want
agree	hope	wish	fail	plan
learn	manage	refuse	expect	need
...	...	...	...	...

Dominoes (set B)				
swimming	having	eating	opening	speaking
standing	sitting	listening	doing	taking
...	...	...	...	...
to lie	to do	to teach	to see	to have
to play	to buy	to get	to go	to visit
...	...	...	...	...

这个游戏叫做“多米诺骨牌”，旨在帮助学生通过配对游戏牌来巩固区分哪些动词后接动名词，哪些动词后接不定式以及哪些动词后两者均可。游戏中分为两类牌，学生需将手中持有的动词牌与被翻开的动名词或不定式牌进行匹配，并用该匹配成功的短语进行造句。该游戏能够帮助学生有效巩固动词的搭配，也能促使学生在造句时关注表达的正确性以及语境的合理性。

为了使游戏更具趣味性，教师可以在 A 牌中加入几张功能牌，譬如跳过牌（*Skip*），学生可以在无牌能匹配的情况下使用它；一旦该牌被打出，下家就失去了出牌机会，而是轮到再下家出牌。又如反转牌（*Reverse*），当学生打出反转牌后，整个出牌顺序将翻转过来。功能牌的加入，无疑是游戏难度上的一次进阶。如何发挥功能牌的最大价值，从而获得最终的胜利，看似简单，实则需要学生具备洞察全局、准确推理的能力。

51 Guess Who He/She Is

Focus: The Simple Present (Affirmative and Negative)

Level: Elementary

Duration: 10～15 minutes

Procedure:

- Prepare slips of paper in advance.
- Ask each student to write six true sentences about himself/herself on a slip of paper. Three

○ 为了避免学生间猜不出纸条的主人是谁，教师在游戏开始前可以举例说明，强调句子需体现出个人特色。

sentences should start with *I*... while the other three should start with *I don't/ am not*...

- Collect the slips and shuffle them in a box.
- Ask students to take turns to take one slip out at random and read out the six sentences that are written on it. The six sentences must be changed into the third person form when being read out.
- Ask the other students to guess who the writer is and state their reasons.

○ 转述过程中若学生出现错误，教师应及时纠错或指定其他学生进行纠错。

Examples:

The sentences written on the slip:	**The sentences read out:**
I am an outgoing girl.	She is an outgoing girl.
I have many friends.	She has many friends.
I am a foodie (who likes eating).	She is a foodie (who likes eating).
I like doing sports.	She likes doing sports.
I am not good at Maths because I don't work that hard.	She is not good at Maths because she doesn't work that hard.
I usually go to school on foot and carry a big bag.	She usually goes to school on foot and carries a big bag.

Discussion:

Student A: Can you guess who she is?

Student B: Well, I think she might be Linda because Linda is sunny and lovely. Also, she shows great talent in sports.

这个游戏叫做“猜猜他/她是谁”，旨在帮助学生进一步巩固一般现在时人称和动词的一一对应及相互之间的转换。通过“我”写、他人转述、大家一起来猜的游戏环节，激发学生主动参与活动的热情，从而增强课堂的有效互动，提升学生最终的学习效果。针对不同程度的学生，教师还可以调整任务难度，譬如要求学生在写6个关于自己的句子时，必须有意识地囊括2个特殊的动词词尾变形，譬如，finish-finishes，study-studies，使其他学生们在转述过程中，再次复习巩固第三人称单数变化规则。此外，教师也可以对6个句子的开头不作要求，只限定时态。从封闭型任务转变成半开放型的任务，更能激发学生的表达欲望与参与热情。

52 Are You Sure?

Focus: Present Perfect Tense

Level: Intermediate

Duration: 15～20 minutes

Procedure:

- Organize the class into four teams (Team A, B, C, D) .
- Prepare 20 sentences that each contains one grammar mistake. Write each sentence on cards numbered 1 to 20 and place them face down on the table.

○ 除了将20个有错误的句子写在卡片上，教师还可以借助幻灯片设置翻卡动画，以此来呈现错误的句子，使游戏进程更省时高效。

- Team A goes first and chooses one card for Team B. When the card is turned over and the sentence is read aloud, Team A needs to decide how many points it would gamble. As each team starts with 100 points, it can bet between 1 to 100 points. If Team B could correct the grammar mistake and state the reason clearly after discussion, the points that Team A has gambled will be added to Team B's total. If not, Team B would lose the amount of points. Meanwhile, Team A is given the chance to do the error correction. If Team A could answer correctly and explain the reason, it gets the points instead.
- Following the alphabetical order, Team B then chooses a card for Team C and so forth.
- The team with the most points wins the game and gets the title of *"Grammar King/Queen"* in the end.

○ 为了增加游戏的紧张感，两队对抗时，攻方可指定守方的某一位同学作答，但每一轮挑选的对象需不同。这样的规则设定可以促使每一个队员都投入到比赛的讨论中。

Examples:

The sentences written on the cards:
1. Have you already talked to him? 2. How long have you bought your mobile phone? 3. I have got my hair cut last week. 4. It's ten years since I moved here. 5. Lucy has been to Tokyo and she will be back in two weeks. 6. Have you ever write a letter in English before? 7. On my way to school, my wallet has stolen. 8. I've ever been to New Zealand, but I want to go there this year. 9. Linda and Judy has recently played badminton together. 10. This is the best film that I ever see. 11. Aaron is a captain and he has left his home for a long time. 12. They know each other since January. 13. I have forgot my Apple ID password, so I can't log into my account. 14. How you have been recently? 15. We have got married for 10 years. 16. I lost my phone and now I feel completely disconnected. 17. I've lived here since most of my life. 18. I watch Kobe Bryant's videos loads of times. 19. Lucas hasn't eat all the chocolates. 20. As the train stops, we can go out now.

○ 教师在准备错误句子时，应基于学生学情，尽可能多地囊括常见的易错点。

这个游戏叫做“你确定吗”，旨在帮助学生总结和梳理现在完成时的常见易错点。该游戏采用了积分赛制，并巧妙地加入了“打赌”环节，看似碰运气，实则展现了对知识点难易程度的准确判断。游戏过程中，学生不仅需要纠错，还需要一并说明这样改的理由，其目的是检测学生对于正误的判断是否有理有据，通过这样的方式，促进学生了解和熟练运用此类语法规则。

此外，游戏结束后，教师还可以要求学生对 20 个错误点进行归纳整理，以此达到举一反三的效果。此类游戏适用于所有语法点的改错训练，以摆脱传统语法练习的枯燥乏味，使课堂焕发新的活力。

53 How Much Do You Know About...?

Focus: The Simple Present and Past Passive
Level: Advanced
Duration: 20～25minutes
Procedure:

- Divide the class into two teams (Team A and B) and each team nominates a team leader. Give students a list of traditional festivals home and abroad, such as *Chinese New Year*, *Lantern Festival*, *Christmas*, *Thanksgiving*, etc. and ask each team to choose one. Then each team is given some time to discuss and share what they've already known about these two different festivals in class. For the uncertain information, they have two days to figure it out through self-learning after class. Meanwhile, each teammate should hand in two or three true statements about the festival that his/her team has chosen. After that, team leaders organize team discussions to select ten statements out of all. The teams then make several statements false by changing one piece of information in each sentence.

○ 游戏分组可 2、4、6、8 偶数倍递增。

○ 每组需准备 10 道判断题。由于节日习俗的复杂多样，教师可以引导学生从以下几个方面出题：如节日的由来、节日的习俗、过去与现在人们庆祝方式的差异等。

- During the game, two team leaders roll the dice. The team with the larger number begins the game first by reading aloud the ten statements one by one. The opposing team should first judge whether the statements are true or false and then guess which part of the sentences is wrong. For each correct judgment, the opposing team scores a point. If the opposing team could repeat the sentences or correct the sentences in the simple present or past passive, the team scores another point. At the end of the game, the team with the most points will be awarded the title of *"Super Brain"*.

Examples:

Chinese New Year, also known as Spring Festival, is the most important holiday in China.			
Some statements about Chinese New Year		**True or False**	**Correct the statements by changing active voice to passive voice**
1.	Eldership send red envelopes with lucky money inside to young generation.	True	Red envelopes with lucky money inside are sent to young generation by eldership.
2.	People do the cleaning and sweeping on the New Year's Day.	False	People aren't allowed to do the cleaning and sweeping on the New Year's Day.
3.	People set off firecrackers to welcome the God of Health on the fifth day of the new year.	False	Firecrackers are set off to welcome the God of Wealth on the fifth day of the new year (by people).
4.	People hide a lucky candy or several candies inside the dumplings.	False	A lucky coin or several coins are hidden inside the dumplings (by people).
5.	...	...	...

Christmas is to westerners what Spring Festival is to Chinese. It celebrates the birth of Jesus Christ.			
Some statements about Christmas		**True or False**	**Correct the statements by changing active voice to passive voice**
1.	Only Christians celebrate Christmas.	False	Christmas isn't celebrated by Christians only.
2.	Every year, America sends a beautiful home-grown Christmas tree to Britain.	False	Every year, a beautiful home-grown Christmas tree is sent to Britain by Norway.
3.	Britain gave the Statue of Liberty to the USA as a Christmas gift.	False	The Statue of Liberty was given to the USA as a Christmas gift by France.
4.	People eat chicken and plum cakes during Christmas.	False	Turkey and plum cakes are eaten (by people) during Christmas.
5.	People call Christmas as Xmas as well.	True	Christmas is also called Xmas (by people).
6.	...	...	...

○ 想要了解更多关于挪威赠送圣诞树给英国这一习俗的缘由，可以登录该网址查阅相关资料：https://norwaytoday.info/culture/why-does-norway-give-a-christmas-tree-to-the-uk-every-year/

这个游戏叫做“你对……了解多少”，旨在帮助学生进一步巩固一般现在时和一般过去时中主动语态与被动语态的转换。该游戏将节日文化的探索融合于知识点的操练，引发学生对不同节日文化的思考。该游戏以学生为主体，从课内到课外，通过学生自学、互相讨论探究来促进课堂的教与学，提升学生自主学习及互相协作的能力。由于该游戏与传统节日文化相结合，因此所操练的时态集中于一般现在时和一般过去时。教师可以改变话题，以满足其他时态下被动语态的练习。

游戏结束后，教师还可以要求学生对课堂讨论的内容写一份总结，所写句子尽可能多地使用被动语态，以此来考察学生对知识点的掌握情况。

54 Action!

Focus: While + Past Progressive

Level: Lower-intermediate

Duration: 10～20 minutes

Procedure:

- Prepare pieces of cards in advance. On each card, write an activity that can be easily and clearly performed, such as *read a book, do your homework, lie on the sofa, watch TV, brush your teeth, wash your face, comb your hair, put your jacket on, drink a cup of hot water, drive a car, ride a bike, play the piano,etc.*
- Give each student one card and ask him/her to keep it secret.
- Ask different students to perform their actions according to their cards. The others watch and guess the action. While guessing, they should use the past progressive to express their ideas. For example, *(I think) you were doing your homework.*
- After most students get familiar with the different activities, divide students into groups of 5～6.

○ 如果学生不清楚卡片上的词组含义，允许学生向教师提问。

○ 该步骤旨在帮助学生熟悉过去进行时的基本结构及卡片上的活动，为之后的游戏环节做铺垫。如果学生程度较好，可省去该步骤。

- Ask one group to stand up and perform the activities simultaneously by hearing the word "Action!".
- Get the other students' attention to reporting on two simultaneous activities by using the sentence pattern: *While... was..., ...was...*
- Repeat the exercise by reporting on other activities once or twice and then move on to the next group.

○ 由于每个小组中有5～6位同学，他们所表演的动作各不相同。因此，同一组的句型操练可重复进行2～3次。

Examples:

Group One	The activities they've got
Student A	make your bed
Student B	hang out the washing
Student C	wash the dishes
Student D	do the ironing
Student E	sweep the floor
Student F	lay the table for meals

Discussion:

Teacher: What were student A and student F doing?

Students: While student A was making his/her bed, student F was laying the table for meals.

○ 在句型操练时，教师需关注学生是否进行了正确的人称转换。如该例中，需将 your 变成 his 或 her。

这个游戏叫做“请开始你的表演”，旨在帮助学生学会用 while 及过去进行时来描述过去同一时间点正在发生的两个动作。在开展该游戏时，教师需注意以下三点。一，在准备游戏卡片时，所选择的词组是易于学生表演的。二，词组中的动词应为延续性动词，而非瞬间性动词。三，教师在给小组发放卡片时，可以有意识将同一话题的词组进行归类并发放给同一小组。如上述样例中所展示的那样，6个词组均为家务劳动。这样做的好处在于，学生们不仅可以操练句型，而且能够复习同一话题的相关词汇。

55 Get a Seat

Focus: Yes/No Questions

Level: Lower-intermediate

Duration: 10～15 minutes

Procedure:

- Prepare some incomplete yes/no questions, e.g. *Are you...? Were you... ? Do you...? Did you...?* Write them on pieces of paper and mix them up in a box.

> ○ 不同时态下的一般疑问句基本结构存在一定差异，因此，教师可以根据教学要求，适当增减游戏中训练的句式。

- In class, pick out one student and ask the other students to take their chairs and sit in a circle. Standing in the middle of the circle, the selected student has to choose a piece of paper in the box. He/she then needs to complete the question with the given structure. When he/she calls out his/her finished question, the rest students should answer it truthfully. For example, if the student asks, "*Did you secretly use your phone to play games yesterday night?*" The rest should answer with "*Yes, I did.*" or "*No, I didn't.*" Those who answer "No" to the question should stand up and change their seats while answering the question. Meanwhile, the one who raises this question should try to grab a seat from those who stand up as well. Therefore, in order to keep students motivated in the game, the one who raises the question is suggested to come up with a question that leads to a negative answer. However, if the student unluckily rasies a question with the rest all answering "Yes, I..." , then he/she needs to change his/her question and ask again. The last one who isn't able to get a seat becomes the next one to stand in the

> ○ 游戏中，可能会出现学生问题问错或答错的情况。这时就需要教师的介入。教师应当暂停游戏，启发学生察觉到表述中的错误，待学生自行修正错误后，继续游戏。

> ○ 为避免学生在游戏中后期出现懈怠，教师可以调整游戏规则，让回答 yes 的学生进行座位交换；或者让每一轮提问的学生在提问时自行决定交换座位的对象，以增添游戏的紧张感。

middle and ask the question. The teacher can continue the game until students have practised most of the sentence structures.

Examples:

Arrange the chairs like this

Sentence structures:
Are you...?
Were you...?
Do you...?
Did you...?
Have you...?
Had you...?
Can you...?
...

这个游戏叫做“抢座位”，旨在帮助学生通过问答互动的方式完成对一般疑问句的操练。游戏中，一部分学生需要根据不同句式的开头补充问句，而其他学生则需要根据问句作答。将不同时态的句子集中呈现于游戏中，是希望学生能够对比异同点。譬如现在完成时和过去完成时的问句中都需使用动词的过去分词，而非动词原型。而抢座位的环节设置，能够使原本枯燥的操练瞬间变得有意思起来。学生们需要仔细聆听问题，在迅速做出反应后，找到可以交换的位置，快速坐下。该游戏使学生课堂内的活动空间得以拓宽，也使学生大脑运转起来。

56 Who Is Speedy Gonzales?

Focus: How Long ...?

It Takes...; It Took...

Level: Lower-intermediate

Duration: 10～15 minutes

Procedure:

- Divide students into groups of 4.
- Review the basic structure of the sentence pattern (*"How long did/does it take... to..."* and *"It took/takes... to...")* through a warm-up. Let students discuss in groups to come up with the answers. Students should use a complete sentence to answer the questions.
- Given a copy of map, each student has 2 minutes to read the information on it.
- Listening to a recording, students need to find out who was the first one to get to the swimming pool with the information on the map. Then students are required to check the answer by using the target sentence patterns.

○ 在设计热身活动的问题时，教师可以有意识地切换时态，并以不同的学科视角考察学生对人文、历史、自然的了解。这样一来增加活动本身的趣味性，二来达到拓宽知识面的效果。如果设计的问题较难，可以将答案中对应的数字以打乱的方式呈现给学生，让学生选出数字并推测出合理的时间单位。

○ 最终的任务完成需要学生对图片上的信息了然于胸，因此教师务必预留足够的时间让学生仔细观察图片。

Examples:

Warm-up
Discuss in groups and answer the questions.
1. How long does it take sunlight to reach the Earth? 2. How long does it take people to travel from Shanghai to Hangzhou by high speed train? 3. How long did it take the Greeks to take control of Troy? 4. How long does it take the Moon to go round the Earth? 5. How long did it take the ancient Chinese to build the Great Wall during the Ming Dynasty? 6. How long did it take the teacher to plan this lesson?

Aaron, Tony and Ashley decided to go swimming after school. Read the map below carefully, listen to the recording, and find out who was the first one to get to the swimming pool. Check your answers in groups.

The map

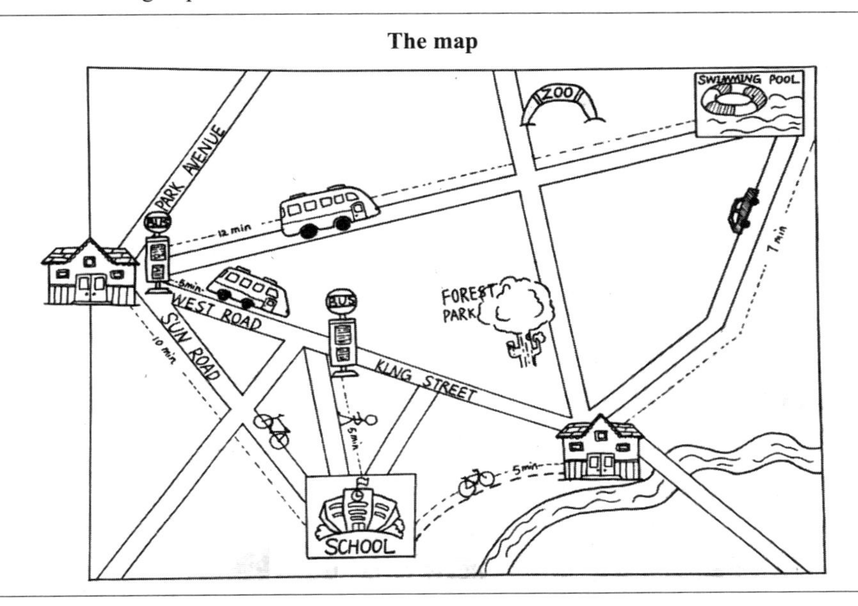

Listening Script:

Aaron, Tony and Ashley decided to go swimming and they left the school at the same time. However, they took different ways to get there. Aaron rode his bike along the river to his house. Then 15 minutes later, his mother took him to the swimming pool by car. Tony rode his bike to his house at the corner of Park Avenue and Sun Road and then waited 3 minutes for the bus, which he took to the swimming pool. Ashley walked to the bus stop in King Street. She waited there for 4 minutes and then got on the bus to the swimming pool.

Possible Discussion:

Student A: How long did it take Aaron to get to the swimming pool?

Student B: It took him 27 minutes to get to the swimming pool.

Student A: Do you all agree with...?

...

这个游戏叫做“谁最快”，旨在帮助学生巩固关于某人花多少时间做某事的句型表达。游戏环节中，学生需要“眼观六路，耳听八方”，将所听所见的信息进行整合，推断出谁使用最短的时间，最先到达泳池；并借助目标句型的问与答，完成情境下的语言内化。语法教学离不开真实的语言情境，只有通过模拟真实的情境，学生才能知其义，晓其用。因此无论是哪一种词法、句法的操练，都建议教师们为学生创造合理的语言交际情境，从而更好地培养学生的语言运用能力。

57 Pick One

Focus: Question Tags

Level: Lower-intermediate

Duration: 10～15 minutes

Procedure:

- Divide the class into groups of 3. Give each group a set of cards. Ask them to shuffle the cards and deal them out evenly.
- The students hold their cards close to their chests so that others can't see them. If they see that the two cards in their hands can go together, they can directly place them face up on the table and make a sentence. They then take turns to pick one card from the student on their right, lay down the matching cards and make sentences. The first one to get rid of the cards wins and the one with the Joker at the end of the game loses.

○ 在游戏过程中，每位学生拿出一对纸牌并且组成一句反意疑问句时，其他学生要留意组成的反意疑问句是否正确，当有错误时，应要求犯错误的学生收回纸牌。

Examples:

They work hard,	don't they?	Let's go to the market,	shall we?
You didn't come,	did you?	He can swim,	can't he?
Give me a hand,	will you?	Few people knew the news,	did they?
These flowers are beautiful,	aren't they?	She can't drive,	can she?

○ 每副纸牌共有51张。教师在制作纸牌时，先准备25句反意疑问句，然后将每句反意疑问句的陈述句与简短问句分开，然后印在不同的50张纸牌上。最后，再单独准备1张鬼牌。

续表

He rarely cries,	does he?	Joanna is a teacher,	isn't she?
Richard shouldn't drive so fast,	should he?	The weather is lovely today,	isn't it?
The trains are never on time,	are they?	Your parents have retired,	haven't they?
The phone didn't ring,	did it?	You won't tell anyone,	will you?
Jennie eats cheese,	doesn't she?	The bus isn't coming,	is it?
I told you,	didn't I?	She will come at six,	won't she?
Peter hasn't done his homework,	has he?	Don't do that again,	will you?
We must go,	mustn't we?	William looks unhappy,	doesn't he?
There is something wrong,	isn't there?	Joker	

这个游戏名为“选一张”，这是一个纸牌游戏，旨在帮助学生巩固反意疑问句。反意疑问句由两部分组成：前一部分是一个陈述句，后一部分是一个简短问句。将反意疑问句的两部分拆开分别印在两张纸牌上，而这两张牌就称为一对。游戏规则是，玩家要轮流从右手边玩家那儿抽取一张牌，将其与自己原本的牌组合，凡是组成一对的牌，就可以丢到桌面上，最先把牌丢光的人为赢家，而比赛最后，谁手里有鬼牌，谁就是输家。因此，这个游戏十分考验学生对反意疑问句的熟悉程度，他们要准确判断手里的陈述句和与之匹配的简短问句以组成反意疑问句，一旦错过，成对的牌也可能会被别人

抽走。这个游戏还考验学生的“演技”，当他们手握鬼牌时，不仅要尽量不动声色，而且还要想方设法让别人抽走这张鬼牌，这也正是这个游戏的趣味所在。在游戏过程中，教师要在一旁仔细观察，留意学生犯的一些错误，将其记录在黑板上，在游戏结束后，给予学生反馈，帮助学生进一步巩固反意疑问句的构成规则。

58 What's the Word?

Focus: Defining Relative Clauses

Level: Intermediate

Duration: 15~20 minutes

Procedure:

- Write down the definition of a word “a place where planes take off and land” on the board and ask the students to guess what the word is. Elicit the word “airport” . Tell the students that they are going to write definitions of the words as clues for a crossword puzzle.
- Divide the class into two groups (Group A and Group B) and give each student a corresponding worksheet. Both groups have the same crossword puzzle, but Group A has the words across and Group B has the words down.
- Working with two or three other students from the same group, the students write down clues for the words on their crossword puzzle using defining relative clauses.

○ 对于一些能力水平较高的学生，可以让他们独立编写线索。对于能力水平低一些的学生，可以让他们以小组形式合作完成。

- After discussion, each student in Group A forms a pair with a student in Group B. They mustn't show their crossword puzzle to their partner. They solve their crossword puzzle by asking their partner for clues to the missing words. They read out the clues they have written for their partner and give more clues if their partner is unable to guess the words. When the students have completed their crossword puzzle, they compare theirs with their partner's to check their answers.

Examples:

Sample crossword puzzle

									[1]A			[2]B								
					[3]P				I			E								
					A		[4]F	I	R	E	M	A	N							
		[5]G	U	E	S	T			P			C								
					S				O			H								
					P				R											
				[6]C	O	M	P	[7]U	T	E	R									
					R			N												
			[8]C		T		[9]M	I	R	R	O	R								
			H					V									[10]H			
			O					E					[11]P				O			
			C		[12]A			[13]R	E	S	T	A	U	R	A	N	T			
			O		R			S					R				E			
			L		M			I					S		[14]P	I	L	O	T	
			[15]A	R	C	H	I	T	E	[16]C	T		E							
			T		H			Y		I										
			E		A					[17]N	U	R	S	E						
	[18]S				I					E										
	[19]W	A	I	T	R	E	S	S		M										
	E									A										
	A																			
	[20]T	E	A	C	H	E	R													
	E																			
	R																			

○ 在设计填字游戏时，教师可以先确定要放入的词，这些词可以是人物、物品、地点等，但必须是学生熟悉的且容易用限定性定语从句来编写线索的。

Sample worksheets:

Group A

1 2
3
4F I R E M A N
5G U E S T
6C O M P 7U T E R
8C 9M I R R O R
10H
11
12A 13R E S T A U R A N T
14P I L O T
15A R C H I T E 16C T
17N U R S E
18S
19W A I T R E S S
A
20T E A C H E R

Clues across

4 a man whose job is to put out fires

5 ____________________

6 ____________________

9 ____________________

13 ____________________

14 ____________________

15 ____________________

17 ____________________

19 ____________________

20 ____________________

Group B

1A 2B
3P I E
A 4 R A
5 S P C
S O H
P R
6 O 7U
R N
8C T 9 I
H V 10H
O E 11P O
C 12A 13R U T
O R S R E
L M I S 14 L
15A C T 16C E
T H Y I
E A 17N
18S I E
19W M
E A
A
20T
E
R

Clues down

1 a place where planes take off and land

2 ____________________

3 ____________________

7 ____________________

8 ____________________

10 ____________________

11 ____________________

12 ____________________

16 ____________________

18 ____________________

这个游戏名为“这个词是什么？”，这是一个填字游戏，旨在帮助学生巩固限定性定语从句。在传统的填字游戏中，玩家只需要根据题目所提供的线索来解题、填词，而这个游戏不仅需要学生根据线索解题，还需要学生编写线索为别人出题。游戏伊始，将所有学生分为两组并分发相应的填字游戏图，两组学生拿到的图上已填入的单词恰好是不同的，学生首先要做的就是用限定性定语从句为这些词编写线索，线索要尽可能简洁明了。完成线索后，拿到不同填字游戏图的两个人为一组，轮流为对方提供线索，帮助对方填满所有的空格。这个游戏让学生既有解题的成就感，又有出题的趣味感，为学生提供了灵活运用限定性定语从句的空间，充分调动了他们的知识储备，有效锻炼了他们的语言组织能力。

59 To Be Good Listeners

Focus: Reported Speech

Level: Advanced

Duration: 15~20 minutes

Procedure:

- Prepare pieces of cards in advance. On each card, write a topic that are familiar to students and easy to elicit discussion, such as *Favourite movie, Hobbies, School activities, Last weekend, An unforgettable trip, Parents' jobs, Public transportation, Changes in your city, Environmental problems, Recent news, etc.*
- Organize the class into groups of four and divide four students into two pairs.
- Give pairs one card each and ask them to prepare a short conversation (four to six-line) in direct speech according to the topic written on the cards. Two minutes is probably enough.

○ 对话长短、学生准备对话的时间以及对话演绎几遍，教师可以根据学生学习水平做调整。

- In each group, one pair acts out the dialogue and the other pair listens (and takes notes if

○ 学生记笔记时，教师需强调所记内容不是整个句子，而应该是关键词组。

necessary), and then briefly retells the dialogue by using reported speech. Teacher can give some verbs for reference, such as *ask, wonder, say, complain, reply, answer, point out, explain, remind, tell, suggest, mention, think, consider, etc.*

○ 使用间接引语复述对话时，需注意时态、人称、语序的变化以及连接词的添加。

- The original pair listens and checks the new version of the dialogue.
- The two pairs exchange the roles and repeat step four and five.

Examples:

Pair A's topic:	The opening ceremony of Tokyo Summer Olympics
Pair A's dialogue in direct speech:	Simon: Linda, have you watched the opening ceremony of Tokyo Summer Olympics? Linda: Yes， from the beginning to the end. Simon: How do you like it? Linda: Well. In my opinion, it is better than expected. But it is less exciting with no fans in attendance. Simon: I agree with you.
Pair B's new version:	Simon asked Linda whether she had watched the opening ceremony of Tokyo Summer Olympics. Linda said she had watched it from the beginning to the end. Simon wondered how she liked it. Linda thought it was better than expected but less exciting with no fans in attendance. Simon agreed what Linda said.

Pair B's topic:	Chinese athletes at Tokyo Summer Olympics
Pair B's dialogue in direct speech:	Lucas: Kitty, who is your favourite Chinese athlete? Kitty: Zhu Ting. Lucas: Oh, really? I am also a big fan of hers. She is really amazing. Kitty: Shall we watch the volleyball games together and cheer for her? Lucas: That's a good idea.
Pair A's new version:	Lucas asked Kitty who was her favourite Chinese athlete. Kitty answered Zhu Ting was her idol. Coincidently, Lucas said he was also a big fan of Zhu Ting's and he thought she was amazing. Kitty suggested they should watch the volleyball games together and cheer for Zhu Ting. Lucas considered it was a good idea.

这个游戏名为做“做好的倾听者”，旨在帮助学生进一步巩固直接引语

改间接引语。该游戏通过模拟真实的对话场景，让学生就某一个话题展开讨论并在听后进行内容转述，是一个集聚挑战与趣味的活动。活动中，学生不仅需要将直接引语改为间接引语，还需要具备讨论话题及获取信息的能力。听后转述，作为上海中考新加入的一项考查内容，无论是对于学生还是教师来说，或多或少都有些陌生。因此，如果能够将此类活动有意识地运用到教学中，不仅能丰富课堂内容，也能有效地培养学生的能力。

在话题的选取上，尽可能做到题材丰富。如上述样例中关于东京夏季奥林匹克运动会的讨论，就考察了学生是否关注热点时事，其目的在于鼓励学生开阔视野，联系社会，从而提升思维的宽度和广度。

60 Line Up

Focus: Asking and Answering Wh-Questions

Level: All levels

Duration: 5～10 minutes

Procedure:

- Before the game, divide the students into groups of equal size. Each group nominates one member to be the observer while the rest will be players. The observers draw lots to decide which group to observe later.
- During the game, the teacher, as the "caller", will give groups a series of instructions. Each group is required to listen carefully, raise wh-questions to get the information they need and then line up in the order as required. For example, if the caller calls out *"Please line up as quickly as possible by the date of your birth"*, the players need to ask each other the question "*When were you born*?" to quickly get the information and line up. Meanwhile, the observers need to monitor the whole process, making sure no one speaks

○ 由于是小组对抗赛，因此教师分组过程中，必须确保每组人数相同。如果遇到剩余 1-2 名学生的情况，可以让他们充当 caller 或 judge 的角色。

○ 在游戏过程中，每一组都会配有一名观察者。他们需在一旁记录组内成员讨论时使用中文的次数以及小组完成任务的时间，同时还需要在小组任务完成后，检查队伍是否按照要求排列，以此确定每组每轮的积分 / 减分。

Chinese. They also have to do the timing and check the lines after the groups are finished. The first team to line up correctly scores three points. The second gets two and the third gets one. The group either speaking Chinese during the discussion or asking the wrong question will lose one point in each round. The game continues until the caller calls out all his/her instructions. The group with the highest score wins the game.

Examples:

Instructions given by the caller
Please line up as quickly as possible...
1. by your height, the tallest goes first. 2. by the time you got up this morning, the earliest at the back. 3. by the times you do sports every month, the most frequent at the front. 4. by the time you spend in doing homework every day, the longest goes first. 5. alphabetically by the city you want to visit.

○ 为了增加游戏的难度，教师在给出指令时，可以对排队顺序作进一步的要求，如左边样例中 ... at the front/back, ... goes first，通过每次变换要求，来促使学生在游戏过程中从始至终专注听取指令。

这个游戏叫做“列队”，旨在帮助学生复习特殊疑问句的结构与用法。该游戏要求学生首先听懂指令，其次快速对指令进行问句转换，接着以提问的方式获取信息，最终按照要求列队。看似简单的任务，实则考察的是学生获取信息和处理信息的综合能力。而特殊疑问句的问与答始终贯穿于整个游戏过程中，使学生在反复的操练中强化该知识点的运用。作为英语学习中的基本句型，特殊疑问句的出现及使用频率极高，因此无论是对于刚接触英语的儿童，还是对具有一定英语基础的小学生、初中生来说，都需要学会使用特殊疑问句进行提问并根据提问作出回答。

该游戏巧妙地运用“问答”方式对所学基本句型进行操练巩固，教师只需根据学生近期所学句型调整训练内容即可。

Part Four

Reading and Writing

（读写）

61 Opinion or Fact Toss

Focus: Distinguishing Opinions Between Facts

Level: Lower-intermediate

Duration: 10～15 minutes

Procedure:

- Before the game, help students distinguish facts between opinions. Provide students with some statements to tell the difference. See examples:

  (O) Basketball is the most exciting sport.

  (F) Zoe has one brother.

  (O) Strawberry ice cream is the best flavor.

  (F) Plants need sunshine, water, and nutrients to grow.

> ○ 准备 10 ~ 15 个句子让学生辨认。让学生总结观点和事实的不同之处（尤其注意阴影部分）。

- Split the class into two teams to compete. Place two baskets or containers for two teams to toss the crumbled paper into. One "Fact" basket and one "Opinion" basket.
- Explain to students that they will be reading a passage (or several). As a team, students should find as many facts and opinions as possible in the passage. See the sample passage:

  My name is Sally White. I am a school girl. I love my school. My school is far from my home. Every day it takes long time to get there. I don't like going to school by bike because the road is not flat. So I go to school by bus or on foot. It takes me thirty minutes to get there by bus and an hour on foot. I hate getting up very early every morning because I have no time for breakfast at home. I often get some donuts for breakfast on the way to school. I love donuts for breakfast. But my mum thinks that donuts are the worst food in the world due to the fact that they are too sweet.

> ○ 所选择的文本既要包括观点又要包括事实。可以准备长文本，也可以准备多个短文本。同时需给每组准备一些纸张。学生阅读文本后，把答案写在纸上。游戏时，学生需要先分享答案，再把这些纸揉成团进行投球比赛。

- Mark a line from where students stand to toss. Students take turns to tell if it is a fact or an opinion and then crumble up the statement into a ball. Stand behind the designated line and toss the crumbled answers into the right basket on the teacher's cue. Teams will earn 1 point for the right answer; 2 points for each crumbled ball that lands in the basket.

○ 此游戏的乐趣在于找对观点或事实只得 1 分，而投进球却可以得 2 分。就算学生答错也仍能投球得分。最后获胜队不一定是答对最多的。可增设多条投球线，每条线得分不同供学生自己选择，以此来增加游戏的娱乐性。

Fact and Opinion Signal Words

Fact	reality, truth, fact, research, news, report, information, proven, etc.
Opinion	great, (dis)like, certainly, feel, think, best, worst, believe, assume, etc.

此游戏名叫“观点还是事实，投球大比拼”，旨在通过投球让学生区分“观点”和“事实”。此游戏同时也为观点类写作做了铺垫。对于低年级学生，教师可以在写作中鼓励学生确立自己的观点并能给出理由来证明，让学生认识到一个有效的观点是由多个事实作为依据的。而对于高年级学生，教师可以帮助学生搭建观点类写作的文章结构（如图），同时可以提供一些说明文、议论文等做文本分析，辅助学生进行写作。

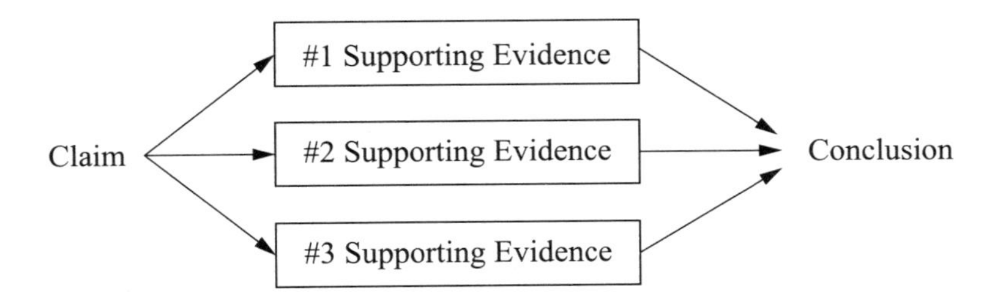

在游戏结束之后，教师需回顾总结文本中的观点与事实的区别，帮助学生提炼一些区别事实与观点的线索词，也可以引导学生在组内讨论并自行总结。分辨观点和事实是锻炼逻辑思维能力的一种重要方式之一，同时也能提高阅读和写作能力。

62 Explore Myself

Focus: Character Analysis

Level: Intermediate

Duration: 10 minutes

Procedure:

- Before getting into character analysis in any text, students may need to spend some time exploring themselves, analyzing various feelings, thoughts, and actions. Providing students with opportunities to explore themselves helps them to imagine how it feels to be the character in the text.
- Distribute a "This is me" template for each student. Ask them to think of one meaningful experience and describe their actions, thoughts and emotions. See the sample template below:

- Working individually, students need to record the information on the template.
- Tell students to focus on the relationships among these elements by asking themselves, "Why do I think or feel in this way?" "What specific reason contributes to my behavior?" . List some guided questions for your students. See the sample response below:

- Have students orally present the template. They need to think about possible reasons and explain the relationships among actions, feelings and thoughts.

○ 学生无需过多描述事件而需重点阐述自己的心理活动、感受以及行为，思考是什么原因导致这样的想法或行为。让学生以分析自己为切入口，进而学会分析人物的性格特点。

- After this game, students are ready to implement this template into character analysis. Discuss the character as a whole person. The teacher needs to help students analyze and understand the motivations and interactions that make up the personality traits of the character.

此游戏叫做“发现自我”，旨在培养分析能力。人物分析多出现于叙事文本以及小说阅读。教师可以在学期开始时引入该游戏。让学生从某事件中分析自己，如自己的性格特点，有哪些内在和外在的因素导致这样的行为，让学生明白分析人物需结合周围环境，同时注意心理活动变化以及感受。之后再带领学生一同分析文本中的人物，提示学生从文中找“证据”、“线索”，通过梳理因果关系来分析人物性格特点。

该游戏同样适用于写作训练，尤其是叙事以及描写题材，能较好地帮助学生丰富写作细节，使叙事或描写更为生动，人物刻画更为立体。

63 The Movie Ticket

Focus: Making Predictions

Level: Intermediate

Duration: 20 minutes

Procedure:

- Make 4 or 5 movie posters. Place them in five different places in the classroom. Each poster should include a picture and the beginning of the plot. See the sample poster below:

Separated from his parents and his siblings by a sudden storm, the young dinosaur Arlo, finds himself miles away from home, with nobody for company but a cave-boy named Spot. Afraid, alone, and hopeless, the unlikely companions embark on a wild adventure in the vast landscapes, bent on finding Arlo's farm up in the Clawtooth Mountain to be safe again. **Will the little Arlo overcome his fears and reunite with his family?**

- Meanwhile, make movie tickets for the class. The tickets are for students to form groups. 4~5 students will have to work on one movie poster. Tell students to match the movie tickets to the right theatre. See movie ticket sample:

MOVIE TICKET

THE GOOD DINOSAUR

○ 学生拿到电影票后，快速找到对应的影院（找海报），组成一个4～5人的小组进行活动。根据实际情况，准备4～5个iPad，在每一个海报点准备一个该电影的预告片，以更好地帮助学生预测。

- Have students observe the caption and read the plot. Ask them to combine the clues in the passage and their own experiences to make predictions of what will happen later in the movie. Distribute worksheets for each group member.

Clues	**Your Experiences**	**Predictions**	**Score:** ______
Arlo feels hopeless because he lost his family in the disaster. Spot helps the dinosaur along the journey.	A Disney movie always includes risks and ends in a positive way. Meanwhile, the protagonist always undergoes some emotional transformations and becomes strong.	Arlo will overcome all the difficulties with the help of Spot and meet his family again.	**3 points** Right On **2 points** Mostly Got It **1 point** Not Close

- Students should first fill in the prediction form individually. They then exchange with other students in the group. Flip over the poster to review the synopsis of the film. Group members need to score each other based on the accuracy.

○ 提示学生在文本中找线索，并结合常识及自身经历做出合理的预测。完成预测后，给学生看完整故事情节（海报背面），组内互评并打分。

此游戏叫做“电影票”，旨在让学生知道预测是阅读语篇重要的技巧之一，以及如何进行预测。需要提示学生，预测不是胡乱猜想，而是根据图文所给的信息以及自身的经验做预测。如游戏中的案例所示，可依据的线索为主人公“遭遇不幸”“沮丧”“伙伴陪伴”等；而经验则是迪士尼电影的一贯主题——“成长”，即主人公遭遇困难后，通过伙伴帮助，相互陪伴、成长，最后结局圆满。根据不同文本，个人经验也可以是积累的常识、知识。

该游戏同样适合低年级的学生。可以选择简短的故事，配上图片让学生仔细观察再做预测，培养逻辑思维能力。而高年级学生需要在阅读文本的过程中，边分析边调整预测，以便更好地理解作者意图。

64 We Need a BRIDGE

Focus: Identifying Cause-and-Effect Relationships

Level: Intermediate

Duration: 10～15 minutes

Procedure:

- Before the game, students need to understand the relationship between events and consequences in order to make logical connections. Familiarize students with the signal word which works as a bridge to link cause-and-effect relationships.
- Create a "cause-and-effect" bridge word list. Print it out in big font and cut it.

Bridge Word List

because	so	as	since	due to	make	cause (verb)	cause (noun)	therefore	as a result

- Prepare 10 pairs of cause-and-effect relationship pictures, one cause correspondents to one effect.

eg.

texting while driving

car accidents

○ 图片旁附上简单的注释帮助学生理解。

- In classroom, along the blackboard, have 10 students stand in line holding 10 words, facing to the audience. Meanwhile, distribute 10 pairs of pictures to the rest of the class randomly.
- Explain the game rules with demonstration. Let students quickly find the

best match. Additionally, the paired group needs to get a "bridge" word to link the cause and effect. First come first served!

○ 教师可以邀请学生一起示范。最先配对成功的可以优先挑选 bridge word，组成一个三人小组。

- In this group of 3 (a cause, an effect and a bridge word), they need to create a sentence showing the cause and effect of the matching pictures.

  e.g. **Texting while driving** causes *car accidents*.

  The cause of *car accidents* is **texting while driving**.

- If time permits, have more groups share the sentences with the class. The instructor may choose signal words such as *due to, make, cause(noun), cause(verb)* to share.
- After this game, have students identify cause-and-effect relationships in the given text with the help of graphic organizers.

○ 分享句子时，三位学生需面对观众，手举图片展示出 cause，effect 以及 signal words 的顺序。目的是说明如何运用 signal words 连接 cause 和 effect。

此游戏叫做"我们需要一个桥梁"，目的是帮助学生通过一些 signal words 辨认出语篇中的因果关系。教师需要帮助学生理解 signal words 就如同桥梁一般连接事件发生的原因以及结果。教师可以在分析文本中的因果关系前开展此游戏，让学生意识到因果关系对于文本理解的重要性，从而理清作者的写作逻辑。等学生熟悉基本概念之后，教师可以提供一些说明文、记叙文或小说节选。因为在文本中，往往一个原因可以导致不同的几个结果，一个结果也可能由不同原因所导致。教师可根据不同语篇类型、难易程度制作不同的 graphic organizer 帮助学生。如：

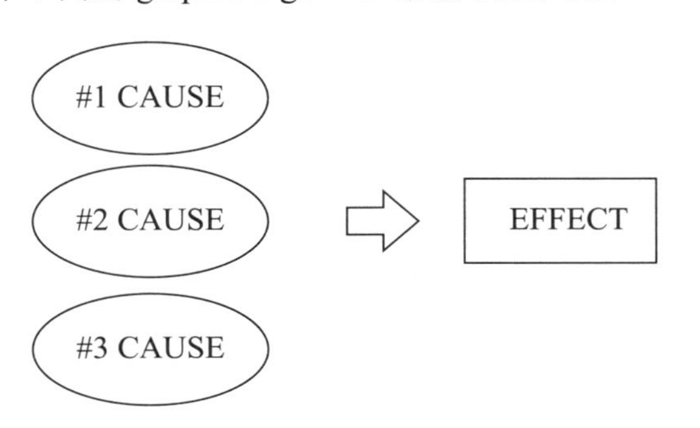

○ 设计一些 Graphic Organizer 来分析，可以更好地帮助学生理解文本脉络，同时教师可以根据学生的语言程度、文本难度，制作个性化表格。通过小组合作或不同形式展开讨论或分析。

65 Whose Desk Is This?

Focus: Making Inferences

Level: Intermediate

Duration: 10～15 minutes

Procedure:

- Before the game, explain to students that making inferences is not a guess or a personal interpretation. It requires textual evidence and what you already know about the topic.
- Take a photo of a random student's desk in your class. Show the picture to the class and have them guess whose desk is this.

Task:

Observe this desk. Then, based on what you can see on the desk, make inferences about who owns the desk.

- Working in groups or in pairs, students need to finish the task by completing this chart.

Evidence:	2 books and an opened notebook; a pencil case; an apple; a ruler; a school bag.
What you already know:	It seems that he/she gets organized for an up-coming maths lesson and an organized person is likely to be efficient.
Your Inference:	This desk belongs to Mark because he is an organized person and he loves maths.

○ 只要学生给出合适的理由证明自己的结论即可。可以多提供几个案例让学生分析，增加趣味性。

- Then have students practise how to make inferences in a reading passage. See the sample passage:

  Billy is a very responsible and considerable neighbor. He is always looking for ways to help out the people who live on his street. During winter, he shovels the driveways of his next door neighbors. During summer, he often mows the lawns for the elderly people who live on his street. He's cautious about how loud he plays his music. He would never want to disturb the neighbors.

  Question: Based on the passage, which of the following is Billy least likely to do?

  A. Have a party at home

  B. Feed a neighbor's cat

  C. Bring in newspaper for a neighbor

- Have students discuss and make inferences by completing the chart. See the sample response:

Textual Evidence:	See highlighted information in the passage.
What you already know:	Having a party usually makes too much noise and will disturb the neighbors.
Inference:	Billy is least likely to have a party at home because he wouldn't want to disturb the neighbors.

○ 阅读时，提示学生先列出文中的相关信息。可以小组合作也可以两两合作。根据学生程度可以调整篇幅难度。

此游戏名叫“这张课桌是谁的？”，旨在训练学生联系上下文理解语篇。推理是阅读的重要技巧之一，不仅考察学生是否读懂语篇，同时需要结合自身理解和知识储备得出一个合理的结论。

该游戏训练学生的阅读推理能力。若直接让学生阅读文本、解读文本会比较枯燥乏味，因此，让学生从“图片观察”过渡到“文本观察”。建议在分析语篇之前开展此游戏，能较好地调动学生的积极性。

66 Tangram Puzzle

Focus: Identifying Supporting Details for the Main Idea

Level: Advanced

Duration: 15 minutes

Procedure:

- Divide students into 4 groups. Each group will get a shape. Each group will need to piece a tangram puzzle according to the shape they get (square, triangle, parallelogram and rectangle).And on each piece illustrates a type of supporting detail.

○ 每个小组都需要将一套七巧板拼图（打印在 A4 纸上，一组一张）分别拼成正方形、长方形、三角形及平行四边形（七块都要用到）。让学生注意到每一块拼图上都有一个英文单词。先让学生理解每个单词的意思，等游戏结束后再揭晓用意。

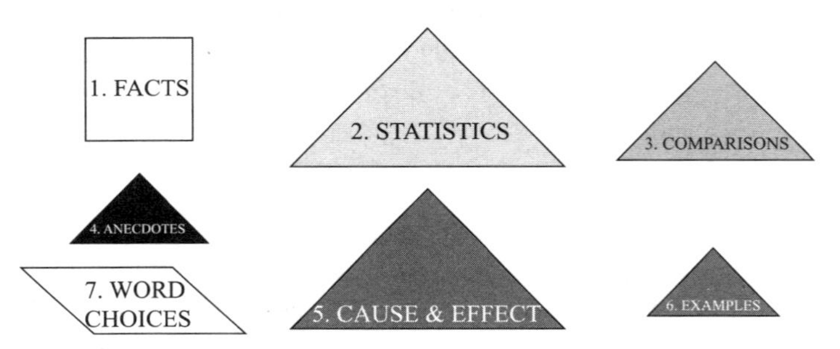

- At the back of each piece of paper, write a line "WHAT TYPES OF SUPPORTING DETAILS DO AUTHORS USE?" . Using as clue, students will put 7 pieces together into the following shapes.

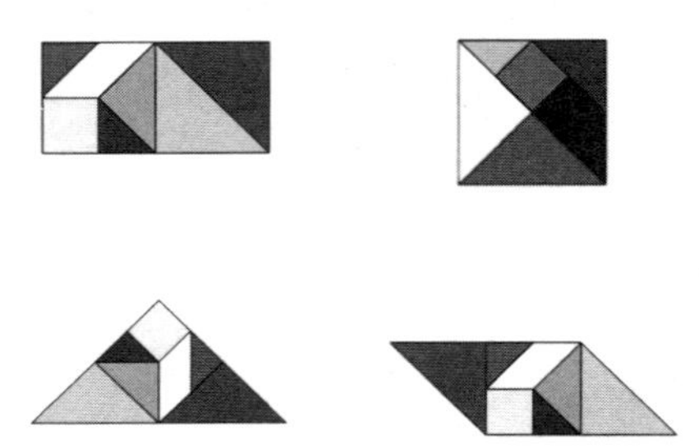

○ 教师在制作七巧板时，在四幅图（见左图）的背后均写上"WHAT TYPES OF SUPPORTING DETAILS DO AUTHORS USE?"作为拼图线索，之后教师再如图裁剪后分别发给 4 组。七巧板拼成后，学生就会看到这个问题，而答案则是各块七巧板上的单词。

- When students finish the puzzle, introduce and explain these 7 ways authors use to support the main idea or the claim. Provide students with examples for practice. For example:

○ 教师解释每一种方法并提供案例让学生练习。可以以小组抢答形式，举起相应的七巧板示意答案。最后提示学生作者可能会同时运用好几种方式来论证观点。

  (1) I once had a Husky. Every day, he'd run out, pick up the newspaper and deliver it to me. He is so smart. (anecdotes)

  (2) My hometown and my university town have many things in common. (comparison)

  (3) According to a survey of 500 citizens, street-cleaning was the city service people liked most. (statistics)

- Remind students that supporting details do not always fit in one category, sometimes writers overlap them and classify them in many different ways.

这个游戏叫做“七巧板拼图”，旨在帮助学生了解作者是如何运用一些论证或说明方法来支撑自己的观点的。该游戏与数学中的几何图形知识相连接，增加了语言课堂的趣味性。

该游戏的重点是让学生了解几种常见的论述方法，对于阅读说明文或议论文很有帮助。对于低年级学生，教师在介绍时需给出例句让学生有更直观的认识，之后教师可以尝试让学生分析文本，找出观点以及对应的论证或说明方法。对于高年级学生，则鼓励他们在写作中针对不同的文体，学会运用一种或多种方式论述自己的观点。

67 Can You Get the Main Idea?

Focus: Identifying Information Words

Level: Advanced

Duration: 10～15 minutes

Procedure:

- In groups or pairs, students will read a paragraph with some words missing and ask if they can still get the general meaning and write a brief summary. See example:

Studies show ________ wear ________ helmet, ________ reduce ________ risk ________ head injury ________. ________ ride ________ neighborhood, you ________ wear ________ helmet. ________ wearing ________ helmet isn't cool, ________ health and safety. ________ without ________ helmet isn't worth ________ injury or death.

Can you get the main idea?

____

○ 引导学生注意这些 information words 的词性（多为动词以及名词）。同时让学生注意标点，因为标点有助于断句，辨识句式，理解大意。

- Ask students what these words are and why they can come up with the main idea by just reading these words. And then show them the original one to check the accuracy.

Studies show that if you wear a helmet, you reduce your risk of serious head injury by 50%. Even if you're only going for a short ride around your neighborhood, you should still wear a helmet. While you might think that wearing a helmet isn't cool, it is essential to your health and safety. Riding your bike without a helmet will add the risk of injury or death.

- Ask students what these missing words are (highlighted words) and why they can be omitted while reading. Explain that the function of these missing words is like glue and decorations, providing connections and adding extra information.

○ 引导学生认识到阴影部分文字大多为形容词、冠词以及连接词等，而剩下的则是关键信息。阅读时，快速识别出关键词能帮助理解。

- Tell students that concentrating on information words helps them to read faster with better comprehension. Divide them into a group of 3～4. Provide several informational texts and ask them to just keep the information words and erase rest of the words just like the given sample.

○ 教师要选择说明文，截取一段即可。提示学生可以用修正带去除部分单词，保留关键词以及标点。

- When they finish, choose random groups to trade the text. Both groups need to guess the general meaning and summarize the main idea.

○ 让小组之间相互交流讨论，共同查看选取的关键词是否能帮助理解，是否包括动词和名词。

After that, they trade back again to check the main idea.

- The teacher may need to check if the selected information words in each group are accurate and helpful.

该游戏名叫“你能读懂大意吗”，旨在让学生知道精准定位关键词能帮助提高阅读速度以及效率。在说明文中，动词和名词大多为关键的信息词，而一些数据、形容词等大多则作为补充的辅助信息，所以教师尽量选取说明性文本。

每组在挑选信息词时，教师应提示学生注意动词以及名词。小组之间交换文本，总结大意，总结完之后交给原始组查看理解上是否与原文有偏差。若有偏差，教师应提供修正的机会，鼓励组内进行讨论，看是由于选择的信息词不准确还是理解不到位所致。在之后的阅读课中，教师可以逐步培养学生在阅读文本时有意识地圈画信息词来提高阅读效率。

68 Make a Chain

Focus: Introducing Paragraph Structure

Level: Elementary

Duration: 10 minutes

Procedure:

- Sitting in lines, students form several groups. Each group will have a piece of A4 paper and make it into accordion folds. See sample:

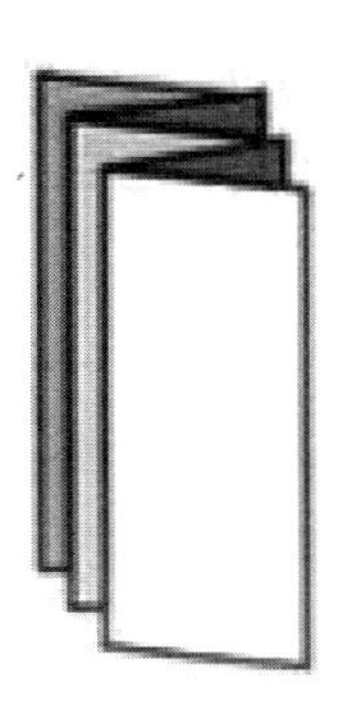

○ 根据每列学生的人数决定几折。每位写完依次往后传。每位同学需按照上一位同学写的内容写。

- Explain to students that they will make a chain. To decide the writing topic, the teacher prepares many writing topics in a container for the first-row students to pull out of. The first student will write a topic sentence; the last student will make a conclusion; the rest of the students in a line, each will write one supporting detail. See the sample response:

○ 第一位学生需要写出主题句确定内容。中间的学生不能重复上一位的理由。最后一位学生需要结合主题句以及细节信息，作出结论。

Topic: Dogs
Dogs are the most friendly pets.(topic sentence)
They make us happy.(#1 supporting detail)
They love us more than themselves. (#2 supporting detail)
They help the blind in their lives. (#3 supporting detail)
Dogs keep us happy and healthy.(conclusion)

- Have each group read their chain, and then swap with other groups to read. Help the class to summarize the paragraph structure. A paragraph structure includes a topic sentence, some supporting details and a conclusion.

该游戏叫做“链接”，旨在帮助学生搭建写作框架。对于低年级英语学习者而言，在写作初期需要为他们搭建一个基本的写作框架，按照这个框架练习不同文体的写作，如叙事、描述、说明以及议论（观点）。在基本框架下训练不同文体可以帮助学生梳理写作思路。

该游戏结束后，建议教师给出不同文体的写作框架指导，并让学生尝试不同文体的写作，让学生有个大致的写作概念。随着之后的深入学习，再慢慢充实写作内容，优化语言。同时，在阅读课中，结合写作基本框架，让学生找出文中的主题句、细节信息和结论，把阅读与写作相结合。

69 A “How to” Guide

Focus: Practising Sequencing for Expository Writing

Level: Elementary

Duration: 20 minutes

Procedure:

- Tell students that they will be making a guide or a manual that teaches people how to do things by themselves instead of asking for help. Provide some situations for students to brainstorm and discuss.

How to give yourself a haircut

How to bathe a cat

○ 在游戏前，教师可以为学生设置一些有趣的情景，如宠物店打烊了，需要自己为宠物洗澡；自己在家剪头发；做三明治等。

How to plan a perfect party

How to mow your lawn

- Working in a group of 4, each group will get a template. They need to decide a "How-to" topic, draw a picture and come up with the process (in a random order). After they finish, they need to swap the template with another group to work on.
- Another group may need to figure out the right order and cut off the steps,then paste steps according to the picture. See the sample response below:

<table>
<tr><td colspan="2">Topic: How to Give Your Cat a Bath</td></tr>
<tr><td rowspan="6">Draw a Picture</td><td>1</td></tr>
<tr><td>2</td></tr>
<tr><td>3</td></tr>
<tr><td>4</td></tr>
<tr><td>5</td></tr>
<tr><td>6</td></tr>
<tr><td colspan="2">Cut the following steps and paste in the right order.</td></tr>
<tr><td>Put her in the water.</td><td>Rub the pet shampoo all over your cat.</td></tr>
<tr><td>Catch your cat.</td><td>Fill a tub with water and prepare a big towel.</td></tr>
<tr><td>Dry her with towel and give her a big hug!</td><td>Wash the suds（泡沫）off your cat.</td></tr>
</table>

○ 该环节也可以练习祈使句的运用。教师需提醒学生每个步骤需用动词开头（如样例中的加粗部分）。

- After the game, they may start to write a short paragraph. Develop a word bank of transitional words that will be used in the writing such as firstly, next, finally, etc. If possible, the teacher may need to provide students with a paragraph form, including a topic sentence, a conclusion and some transitional words. Have students write independently to fill in the form to write their own paragraphs.

○ 教师可以引导学生总结连接词，也可以在写作前直接提供给学生。此外，根据学生实际情况，教师可以为低年级学生提供写作模板。

这个游戏叫做“完成一份指南”，旨在帮助学生明白一篇好的说明文需要提供详细的解说。该游戏让学生思考并列出完成某任务的正确步骤，进而完成一个说明性文本的写作。在列步骤之前，引导学生思考需要准备的物品，如游戏中的案例“如何为宠物洗澡”所示，需要事先准备毛巾、沐浴露，最后可能还需要一些零食作为奖励等。鼓励学生积极讨论，发散思维，关注细节。在写作过程中，可根据学生情况，为学生提供写作模板。

也可以结合祈使句以及连接词的教学开展这个游戏。

70 Folding Jackets to Save Space

Focus: Writing a Topic Sentence

Level: Lower-intermediate and above

Duration: 15 minutes

Procedure:

- Tell students that they will have a competition about how to fold an out-door jacket for travelling. The winner should neatly fold the jacket according to the given instruction in the picture. See the sample picture below:

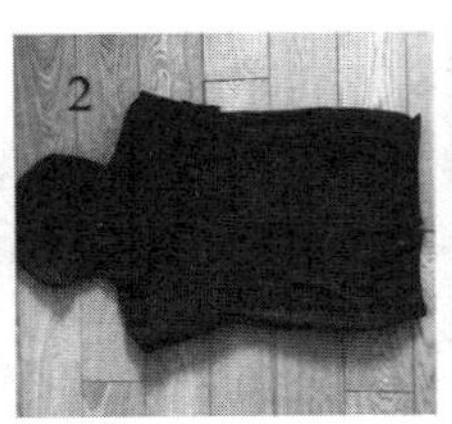

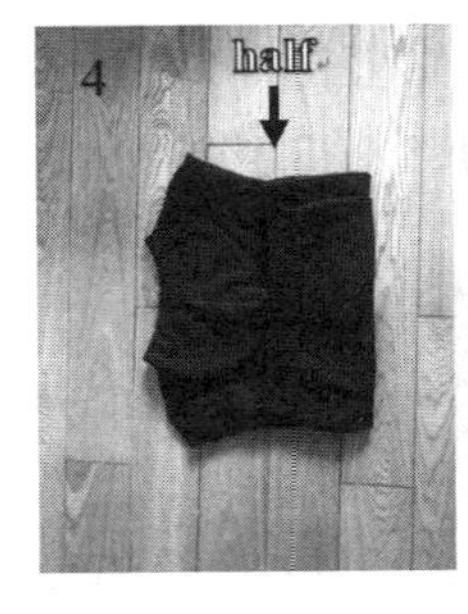

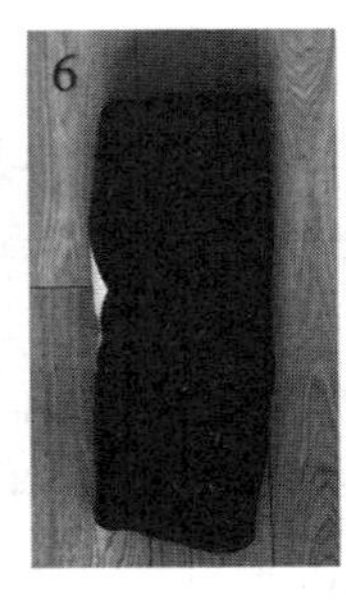

○ 为方便教师操作，游戏中可以使用学生校服，也可以让学生事先带一件外套。教师仅给学生展示图片，学生必须按步骤叠衣服。最后成果和图片一样方可获胜。

- Tell students they need to create a topic sentence with the given supporting details. Explain to students that a topic sentence has a controlling idea with author's attitude or opinion.

Read the caption, fill in the blanks with the first letter and write a topic sentece according to the supporting details. **Topic Sentence**:________________________
Supporting Details 1. Laying on the f____surface and straight it out.
2. Folding both s____over to the other s____.
3. Taking the h____and fold it over.
4. Taking the bottom and fold it over to h____of the jacket.
5. Folding the out-door jacket i____ of the opening.
6. Making it into a pillow to s____ space for travelling.

○ Answer Key
1. flat
2. sleeves, sides
3. hood
4. half
5. inside
6. save

- Have students read the supporting details again. Ask students to highlight the key information in the supporting details for composing a strong topic sentence(See the highlighted words in the sample above).
- Have students write and share in groups. The teacher might need to examplify what a strong topic sentence looks like "How to fold out-door jackets to save space for travelling". Explain to students that through highlighted words, we know it is a thick outfit but not any random clothes; also the context is about how to save space in a suitcase for the purpose of travelling. All theses details help students to compose an effctive topic sentence.

○ 教师需让学生关注到一些重要细节，如是一件较厚的外套，而不是别的衣物；该写作目的是为了节省旅行箱空间去旅行而不是日常整理。

该游戏名叫"如何叠衣服节省空间"，旨在让学生了解主题句的特点，并学会根据细节信息总结提炼出主题句。整理衣物是一项生活必备技能，教师可以提供情境，如去旅行需打包衣物，进而让学生思考如何做才能节省旅行箱的空间，装下更多的东西。课后教师还可以让同学示范更多的整理衣物小妙招，活跃写作课气氛。

此外，这个游戏还考察了学生的概括能力。教师需强调主题句在文中的重要性并列举其特点，必要时给学生提供检查清单，让学生写完主题句后根据检查清单在组内互评、提出修改意见。若是低年级的学生，教师也可以给出几个选项让学生辨别哪一句才是有效的主题句并说出理由。

71 Roll a Fable

Focus: Narrative Writing

Level: Intermediate and above

Duration: 35~40 minutes

Procedure:

- Read a fable or two such as *The Wind and the Sun* or *The Tortoise and the Hare* with the students and ask them to conclude the features of a fable.
- Give each student a dice and a worksheet.

  Sample worksheet:

Roll	Character	Setting	Moral
⚀	Lion	In a forest	One good turn deserves another.
⚁	Rabbit	In a house	A bird in hand is worth two in the bush.
⚂	Donkey	In a village	A friend in need is a friend indeed.
⚃	Fox	On a farm	It's no use crying over spilt milk.
⚄	Bird	By a river	A stitch in time save nine.
⚅	Fish	In a desert	Too many cooks spoil the broth.

○ 该表为学生确定了寓言故事的三大要素：人物、背景和寓意，人物以动物为主，背景以地点为主，寓意以谚语为主，目的是为了让学生能借此加深对这些谚语的了解，并运用到之后的写作中。教师可按需对该表的内容进行调整，如将右栏的寓意改为情节，让学生根据情节自定寓意。

- Each student rolls the dice three times to determine the character, setting and moral of their fable. The students then write their own fable. The moral can't directly appear in their

○ 游戏过程中，学生掷三次骰子，依次决定故事的人物、背景和寓意，一旦确定则无法更改。游戏只提供了一个人物的选择，因此，学生还可以自由地选择增加人物，以丰富故事内容。

writing.

- When the students have finished, collect up the fables, give each fable a number and pin them to the wall.
- The students go round the class, reading the fables, figuring out the three elements of each fable and voting for top 3 fables.

No.	Character	Setting	Moral

○ 学生在看完所有的寓言故事后，选择三个最好的寓言故事，将对应信息填入表格中。

这个游戏名为"'掷'出一个寓言"，旨在使学生充分了解寓言故事的文本特点以及学会编写寓言故事。游戏开始前，先以学生熟悉的寓言故事作为引入，让学生归纳总结寓言故事的三个文本特点：一，文本叙述了一个故事，因此属于记叙文；二，由于情节皆为虚构，故常以拟人化的动物或事物为主人公；三，故事虽短，但具有教育意义，让读者能从中悟到一定的道理。

分析完三要素后，学生进入尝试编写寓言故事的环节。这个游戏的趣味在于学生需要通过掷骰子来决定故事的人物、背景和寓意，这也让许多无从下手的学生能快速投入到写作中去，学生可以尽情发挥自己的想象完成故事创作。考虑到学生水平存在差异，该游戏可以让学生独立完成，也可以两两一组合作完成。

游戏结束后，将学生的作品收集起来张贴在墙上，让学生投票选出三个最好的作品。这时，学生可以转换成读者视角来审视伙伴们编写的寓言故事，在互相学习的过程中反思自己的故事是否有不足之处。

该游戏不仅适用于寓言故事的写作，也适用于其他记叙类文体的写作，如童话故事、小说等，通过游戏，学生可以更加明确故事类文本的基本构成要素，如人物、背景、情节等。通过游戏，学生也能提高写作兴趣，锻炼写作能力，培养创造力。

72 Can You Recognize Your Pistachio（开心果）?

Focus: Figurative Language—Similes and Metaphors

Level: Lower-intermediate and above

Duration: 15 minutes

Procedure:

- In a group of 3～4, students will get a pistachio. Tell them they will be observing a pistachio before describing it.
- Give them some time to closely observe the pistachio. Then fill in an observation form based on what they see or touch. The teacher will collect all the pistachios and line them up on the desk. Ask students to recognize their own pistachio according to the record in the form, and then take it back to the group.

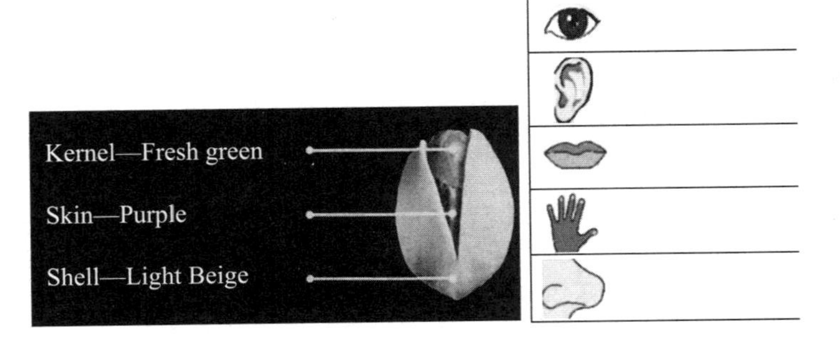

○ 让学生3～4人一组观察一颗开心果，关注一系列感官信息并记录在观察表上。除了用文字记录，学生也可以用图画的方式记录信息来帮助他们辨认出自己的开心果。

- Introduce figurative language—similes and metaphors. Tell students they will be using "imagination" to describe the pistachio. The teacher might need to give examples of the differences between similes and metaphors.

  For example:

  (Simile) Jasmine is like a diamond in the rough.

  (Simile) Rena is as quiet as a mouse.

  (Metaphor) Jill is the apple of my eye.

  (Metaphor) He is such an angel!

○ 根据实际情况，可以提供一些例句让学生辨认或是让学生造句。

- Working in groups, students need to come up with some similes and metaphors of their own to describe the pistachio or any idea that associated with the pistachio. The key point is they need to explain the common ground that the two objects share. See the sample response:

The pistachio looks like a flower bud, ready to bloom.

He put on a pistachio smile with a big open mouth.

○ 无论是明喻或是暗语，造的句子需要包括相应的解释，能够让读者明白两者之间的相似之处（参考阴影部分）。提示学生若没有划线部分，读者无法理解两者之间的联系。

此游戏叫做“你能认出你的开心果吗？”，旨在培养学生的观察能力和联想能力。无论何种写作内容，都需要对细节进行观察以及描写，特别是在叙事性和描述性写作中，除了细节描写外，还需一定的想象力以及生动的语言让习作富有生命力。

此游戏分成两个步骤。首先是让学生对物体进行仔细观察并客观描写。观察的过程是对物体熟悉的过程，必不可少。其次再让学生发挥想象去描述。教师可以根据实际情况，结合其他语言点进行写作练习。

73 Three Little Pigs

Focus: Point of View—Perspectives

Level: Intermediate and above

Duration: 20～25 minutes

Procedure:

- Help students understand that people can have different interpretation on the same topic from different perspectives. In pairs or groups, provide students with several examples to brainstorm.

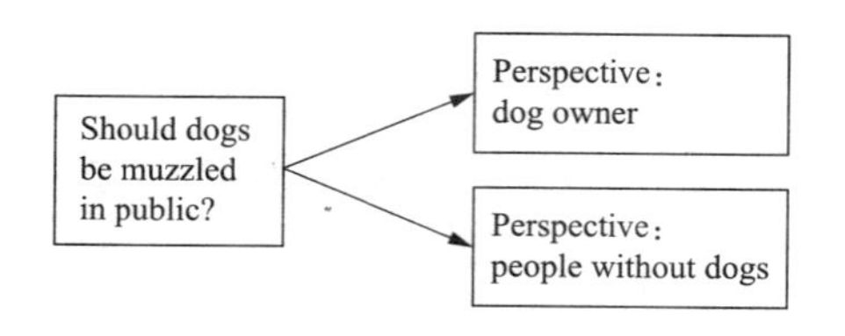

○ 可以多给学生几个讨论话题，学生只需列出有关同一个话题的两个不同角度即可，无需展开阐述，目的是为了让学生知道看问题立场不同观点就会不同。

- Go through *Three Little Pigs* with students (the story is told from the perspectives of pigs). Read the story told from the perspectives of the wolf by Jon Scieszka[1]. See a passage from *The True Story of the Three Little Pigs*.

Way back in once upon a time, I was making a birthday cake for my dear old granny. I had a terrible sneezing cold. I ran out of sugar. So I walked down the street to ask my neighbor for a cup of sugar. Now this neighbor was a pig. And he wasn't too bright either. He had built his whole house out of straw. Can you believe it? I mean who in his right mind would build a house of straw? So of course the minute I knocked on the door, it fell right in. I didn't want to just walk into someone else's house. So I called, "Little Pig, Little Pig, are you in?" No answer. I was just about to go home without the cup of sugar for my dear old granny's birthday cake.

○ 教师可以用不同方式来演绎故事，如多媒体播放或指定学生朗读。需让学生注意阴影部分。

- Distribute worksheets and fill in this table, comparing what is different between the "wolf" version and the "pigs" version. See sample worksheet:

○ 小组讨论时，提示学生需从不同立场来分析。可将故事的起因、经过、结果作为脉络，或是从人物性格特点出发，鼓励学生发散思维。

- Provide students with a list of fairy tales or stories. Have students choose one of them and tell from a different point of view. For example, try to tell *Snow White and the Seven Dwarfs* from the perspective of the step mother.

① Jon Scieszka. *The True Story of the Three Little Pigs*. Viking Children's books.1989.

○ 可以让学生抽签决定，也可以自由选择故事。学生以小组合作形式讨论并完成写作任务。教师尽量选择耳熟能详的故事，内容也不限于英美故事，如可以选择孙悟空三打白骨精的故事，学生可以从反面人物的角度来叙述。提示：无需改编故事情节，而是从不同的人物角度讲述相同的故事。

此游戏名为“三只小猪”，旨在让学生理解写作的不同角度。活动前，教师可为学生提供不同体裁的文章，包括不同的小说节选，帮助学生充分理解“视角”。在活动过程中，通过对比两个故事的起因、经过、结果，帮助学生理解“狼”视角和“小猪”视角的差异。在写作过程中，教师应鼓励学生思维创新，选择有新意的视角。

该游戏鼓励学生批判性地看待问题。若从不同的视角审视作品，读者就会有不一样的解读和体验。写作课堂不仅需要在形式上创新，同时在内容上也应鼓励学生多角度思考。

74 Writing Purpose Spinner

Focus: Author’s Writing Purpose—Persuade, Inform, Entertain

Level: Intermediate and above

Duration: 20～25 minutes

Procedure:

- Before the game, make sure that students understand that the purpose of writing is to provide factual information, to influence or to convince, to entertain. Helping students to identify the three different purposes of writing is a key aspect because it allows students to build on and clarify the concept of "who is your writing audience".

- Tell students they will be making a Writing Purpose Spinner and keep it for the whole semester.
- Distribute Writing Purpose Spinner worksheets and clips. Explain three writing purposes (persuade, inform, entertain) and ask students to write on the spinner. Instruct students to make a spinner according to the following steps:

○ 介绍完写作目的之后，让学生把三个目的分别写在旋转卡片上，让学生美化自己的旋转卡片。

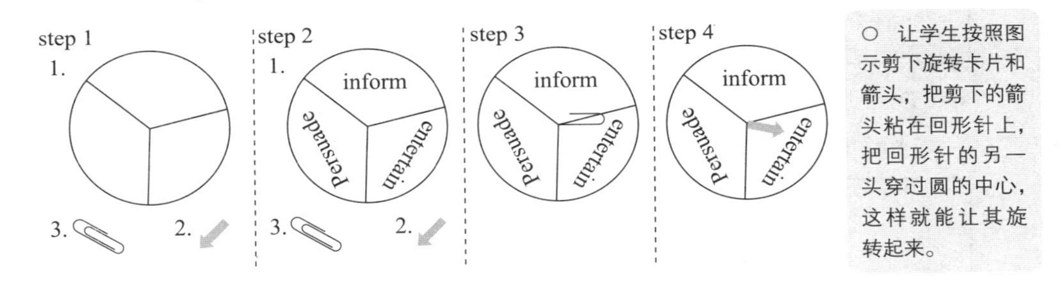

○ 让学生按照图示剪下旋转卡片和箭头，把剪下的箭头粘在回形针上，把回形针的另一头穿过圆的中心，这样就能让其旋转起来。

- On the slides, show some statements for students to identify author's purpose. For example:

  (1) The boys and girls spent the entire day playing in the park. The weather was nice that day and they had fun. (**to entertain**)

  (2) T-shirts for sale! We have a large selection of T-shirts. Our shirts are of high quality. You'll love having one! (**to persuade**)

  (3) Calligraphy is a form of a traditional handwriting that uses a special pen. (**to inform**)

○ 可根据学生程度以及课时安排设计 10 ~ 15 个句子让学生练习。

- Have students determine the author's purpose for each statement. Use spinners, ask them to move their arrow so it points to the right purpose and hold it up in the air to show. Meanwhile, ask students to provide clue words or phrases to support their answers. (highlighted words)

○ 对每一个句子，学生需要阐述通过哪些词来辨认出作者的写作意图。

- Prepare a box with different types of writing. Have students pull a topic from it and start to write. The purpose is to have students determine the purpose of the topic and have some fun. See the sample below:

Topics for Writing Purpose				
why you should brush your teeth	a poem	a movie poster	a complaint letter	a joke
how to make a brownie	a history	a fairy tale	a blog	a perfect weekend
a news report	a manual	a birthday invitation	a rule of a game	a post card

○ 根据班级人数，准备一些题目（可重复），剪下放进盒子。让每位学生抽签来决定写作任务。篇幅根据学生水平而定。

- Distribute writing worksheets for students to work on the task, either in class or as homework. (See Sample)

A Movie Report

Purpose: To ________

Title ________

Underline the clue words or phrases

____

____

____

____

____

○ 根据不同体裁，学生可以选择不同写作方式。若是海报或广告，可以用个性化方式呈现，但必须说明目的并划出线索词。

此游戏叫做“写作目的旋转卡”，学生通过自己制作旋转卡片来了解不同的写作目的。无论中文写作还是英文写作，在动笔之前需确定文体以及写作目的，之后融合自身经历与读者进行连接。此游戏的另一个重要目的是通过让学生了解不同的写作目的来认识不同的文章体裁。

阅读是写作的基础。在阅读中学生若能辨认不同体裁的文本，也就能轻而易举地揣摩出作者的写作意图。因此，这个游戏也可以在阅读课中使用，让学生辨认不同文本以及写作目的，从而达到阅读与写作相辅相成的理想状态。

75 No More Messy Student Desks

Focus: Supporting Opinions with Reasons

Level: Lower-intermediate

Duration: 15 minutes

Procedure:

- Given 5 minutes at the beginning of the lesson, each student needs quickly tidy up and organize the classroom desk, including the storage for books and supplies.
- Then the teacher asks all the students to walk around in the classroom and choose some organized desks. Interview those students to share organization tips and the reason why they like to keep their desks organized.

○ 教师可以自己采访被选中的学生，也可以安排学生采访。学生分享自己整理桌子的心得以及为什么喜欢把桌子整理干净。

- Tell students they will be writing a paragraph about "why should we keep desks organized?" .
- Have students work in groups and distribute graphic organizers for brainstorm. See the sample worksheet below:

○ 首先，小组一起设计一张整理课桌的规划图，包括书本、文具如何摆放，以及桌肚里如何分类摆放不同学科的课本、作业等。其次，想出 3 个为什么需要整理课桌的理由。学生也可以设计自己的规划图。预留一些时间让学生展示交流。

- Ask students to write a paragraph including three parts. Make sure they understand what a paragraph must contain:

  (1) A main idea expressed in a topic sentence.

  (2) Three reasons stated as supporting details.

  (3) A closing sentence connected back to the topic sentence.

- For the beginners, the teacher may need to provide template to help students. See the sample template below:

> **Keep My Desk Organized**
>
> Students should learn how to manage and organize their classroom desks. First, ____________________.
> Secondly, ____________________.
> Last but not least, ____________________.
> Therefore, learning how to keep the desk organized leads to efficient work without wasting time.

该游戏名叫“把课桌整理干净”，通过结合劳动教育，既培养了学生的独立能力以及良好的学习习惯，改善了班级公共环境，也让学生了解如何撰写一个段落，如何组织观点和理由。

学生需要给出自己的观点以及支撑观点的理由。“理由”可能是写作难点，所以通过动手整理以及小组讨论等方式，为学生提供思路。根据学生情况，教师可以选择是否提供模板。模板的设计可以根据教学内容进行调整。教学内容可以是如何写 Topic Sentence 或 Transitional Words 等。对于高年级学生，教师可以不用提供模板，可以尝试“三段式”写作，包括 Introduction、Body Paragraph 以及 Conclusion 的写作训练。

76 Creating My Own Symbol

Focus: Enhancing Structural Cohesion in Narration

Level: Advanced

Duration: 30 minutes

Procedure:

- Before the game, explain to students what SYMBOLS are in literature. Use Chinese poetry to help students understand. Ask students to identify one symbol in each poem and interpret these symbols. See the sample worksheet and response below:

> ○ 首先学生需要明白何为象征意义。象征意义大多是由具体事物表现某抽象概念，如玫瑰（象征爱情）、鸟（象征自由）等，并让学生尝试自己举例。

Task: Identify one symbol in each poem and what do these items symbolize in Chinese cultural values?

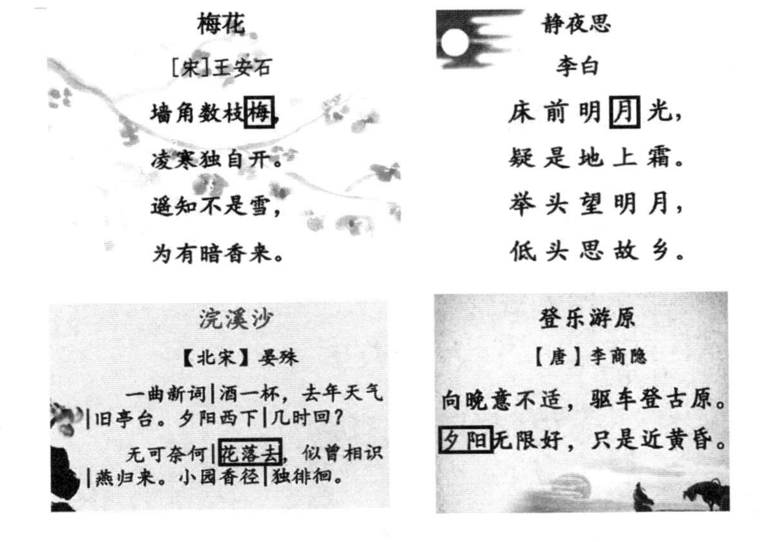

(Answers may vary)

Plum: value of endurance, inner strength, courage, etc.

The Moon: a message of homesickness, etc.

Falling Flowers: often refers to a mood; wonderful things would fade away despite of best efforts, etc.

Sunset: sentimental, sorrowful and a sense of loneliness, etc.

> ○ 让学生关注到中西方文化的差异，可以以“月亮”为例，列举一些中外文学作品或让学生作为课外拓展研究课题。

- Tell students that writers will REPEAT the symbol several times in a story for the purpose of creating atmosphere, developing the plot or reinforcing the theme, etc.

> ○ 象征意义的重复出现是一个很重要的文学手法，有渲染情绪、推动情节发展以及点明主旨等重要作用。可以以学生熟悉的歌曲或电影为例来说明，如重复出现的歌词、台词、物体、场景等。

Therefore, REPETITION is an important literary device that is used in many areas—art, music or movies, etc. Provide students with some examples to discuss, such as repeating lines in a song; reoccurring objects in a movie or story. See the examples below:

○《红楼梦》中“花”是重复出现的意象之一。如黛玉葬花、黛玉创建诗社写有关“花”的诗句等。引导学生讨论“花”在小说中的象征意义是什么？“花”与黛玉之间是什么关系？黛玉为何偏爱花？这些描写对揭示主旨有何帮助？

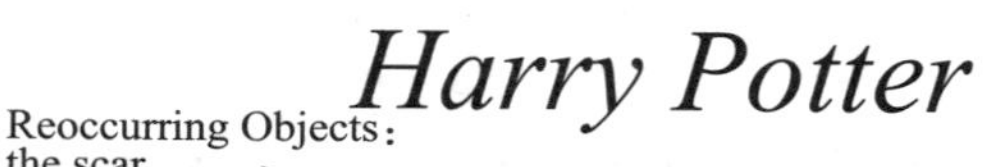

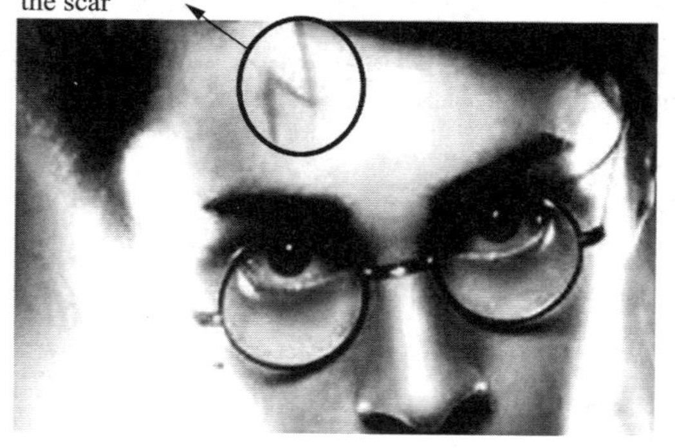

○ 电影《哈利波特》中男主角头上的伤疤重复出现。每一次出现都预示着危险的降临，从而推动着整个故事情节的发展。引导学生思考深层含义，如伤疤的由来，哈利为何每次都能战胜伏地魔？是什么力量支持着他？

- Encourage students to discuss in groups and come up with more examples of reoccurring symbols and be able to illustrate the importance in the context.
- After they understand that repetition of symbols makes the writing highly “structural and developed”, tell them to create their own symbols in the story and REPEAT the symbols in the beginning, middle and the end.

Title: My First Basketball Game

Theme/Mood: The spirit of perseverance.

My Symbol: A pop of sunlight.

My Interpretation: hope, positiveness, emerge from a difficult time.

Ready to insert your symbol in the beginning, middle and end!

Beginning	Middle	End
I saw **a pop of sunlight** on a cloudy morning on the way to regular basketball training.	I saw another **pop of sunlight** when I was worn out during the training but I stayed positive and pushed myself to continue.	I was chosen to be in a basketball game. I saw **a pop of sunlight** right before the game started.

○ 此任务单旨在让学生在记叙文中插入意象，通过重复达到渲染情绪、点明主题的目的。在意象的选择上教师可以先提供一些例子帮助学生打开思路。

这个游戏叫做“创造我的象征符号”，旨在帮助学生了解文学作品中的象征意义并尝试运用到叙事文的写作中。该游戏融合了中国传统文化的教学以及中美文学对比，帮助学生意识到语言的学习是相通的。

该游戏的重点以及难点是让学生明白象征的意义及其在文中重复出现的用意，象征手法目的在于推动故事情节发展、渲染情绪，最终揭示主题思想，因此对文学作品中重复出现的对话、场景描写、意象等应引起重视。在叙事文中多次插入意象可以起到串联全文、完善叙事文写作结构的效果。

对于理解有困难的学生，教师可以提供一些象征意义的例子供他们选择，如“飞翔的鸟”“下雨”“落叶”等；学有余力的学生则可以根据自己的故事需要创造别出心裁的象征意象。教师需提醒学生在创造意象前首先需确定想要表达的主旨及想渲染的情绪，再结合相吻合的象征意义，这样才能起到提纲挈领、呼应全文的作用。

77 Life Cycle of Wild Plants

Focus: Writing a Report

Level: Advanced

Duration: 20～30 minutes

Procedure:

- Tell students that they will need to conduct a report on how plants grow for a biology class. Introduce what a REPORT is. And then explain to students that some plants are planted by people while others can grow on their own. Help students connect to what they have learned in biology lesson with some vocabulary words.

○ 游戏前教师先介绍什么是报告，同时和学生一起讨论有关植物生长的背景知识，如何为光合作用，植物生长需要哪些因素等。确保学生理解这些词汇（游戏中将会涉及）。

Do You Know These Words?

seed(s)	roots	shoot	flower bud	leaves	flower	seed head

- Working in a group of 4, each group will have a plant-growth worksheet（in random order）. Ask students to label the items in the picture with vocabulary words listed above. See the sample worksheet below:

- Distribute life-cycle worksheet. Cut the 4 pictures and put them in the right cycle order. See the sample below:

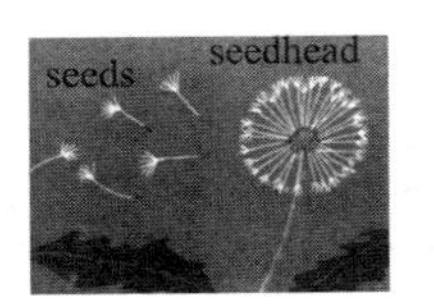

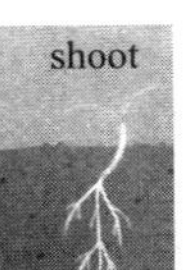

Life Cycle of Wild Plants

○ 教师也可以在黑板上事先准备好图示。可以手绘，也可以做成海报，让学生贴在黑板上展示。

- Distribute a report worksheet. Tell students that a typical report would include such sections, see the sections in the worksheet:

TITLE:
INTRODUCTION:
PROCEDURE & RESULTS:
DISCUSSION/CONCLUSION:

○ 提示学生 Introduction 应包括背景介绍以及研究目的等；Procedures & Results 应按照植物生长顺序进行描述，并需提到生命周期；Discussion/Conclusion 应包括植物生长所需要的因素或光合作用等。根据学生程度，板块内容可以有所调整。

- Explain each section to the students. Ask each group to discuss what information they need for each section and share it in the class with teacher's guide.

- Before writing, teachers can model each section for students or provide them with some report samples. Remind students that writers should stay objective when conducting a report.

这个游戏叫做“植物的生命周期”，旨在通过这个游戏指导学生如何撰写一篇报告。该游戏同时又与生物课所学的知识相结合，对学生来说不难理解，也较为新颖。

在语言层面，学生可能会面临困难，如“怎样用英语描写植物生长过程”“撰写报告如何措辞”等。教师需为学生做好语言铺垫，可以为学生提供一些词组或句子如“fall on the soil”，“roots grow down”，“open into a flower”，“the flower dies”，“a seed head is left”等。提示学生描写时用一般现在时，报告的措辞需保持客观，可根据实际情况融入被动语态的运用等。

78 Sensory Rotation Stations

Focus: Descriptive Language—Five Sensory Descriptions

Level: Advanced

Duration: 20~30 minutes

Procedure:

- Before the game, introduce students to the characteristics of descriptive writing (often quoted as “Show, don’t tell”). An effective descriptive paragraph includes rich sensory details such as vision, hearing, smell, taste and touch to create vivid mental image in the reader’s mind. Additionally, descriptive language demands various sentence structures to add rhythm and energy.
- Provide students with a scaffold for language support. Students will explore how to place adjectives, adverbs or verbs in the beginning of a sentence as introductory phrases to avoid too much “telling” . See the details provided in examples:

Introductory Phrases—Various Sentence Beginnings		
Adjective	Single opening adjective	**Hungry**, Thomas ate two portions of meat.
	Multiple opening adjectives	**Violent and brutal,** the tiger devoured the badger.
	Opening adjective phrase	**Scared to death,** Scout ran all the way home.
Adverb	When	**Overnight,** Jem stared at the smoking hole in the yard.
	Where	**Next to the slides**, the swings creaked.
	How	**Quickly,** George rushed to the dining-room for breakfast.
	Multiple opening adverbs	**Then, slowly,** she went in the back door without a word.
Verb	-ing	**Feeling intense pain**, he locked himself inside the bedroom.

○ 该游戏要求学生变化不同句式来描写。可以尝试把形容词、动词、副词前置于句首，而非使用主谓宾结构。在游戏前教师可以先开展一些相关句型练习帮助学生熟悉句型，让学生了解到描述性写作不仅需要结合“五感”描写，同时语言上也应生动。

- Arrange the class into 5 groups. Make 5 sensory posters and pin them on the wall, making sure to scatter them around the classroom. Prepare 3~4 marker pens for each sensory station (see classroom setting). Also, make a Word Bank for students (see Word Bank).

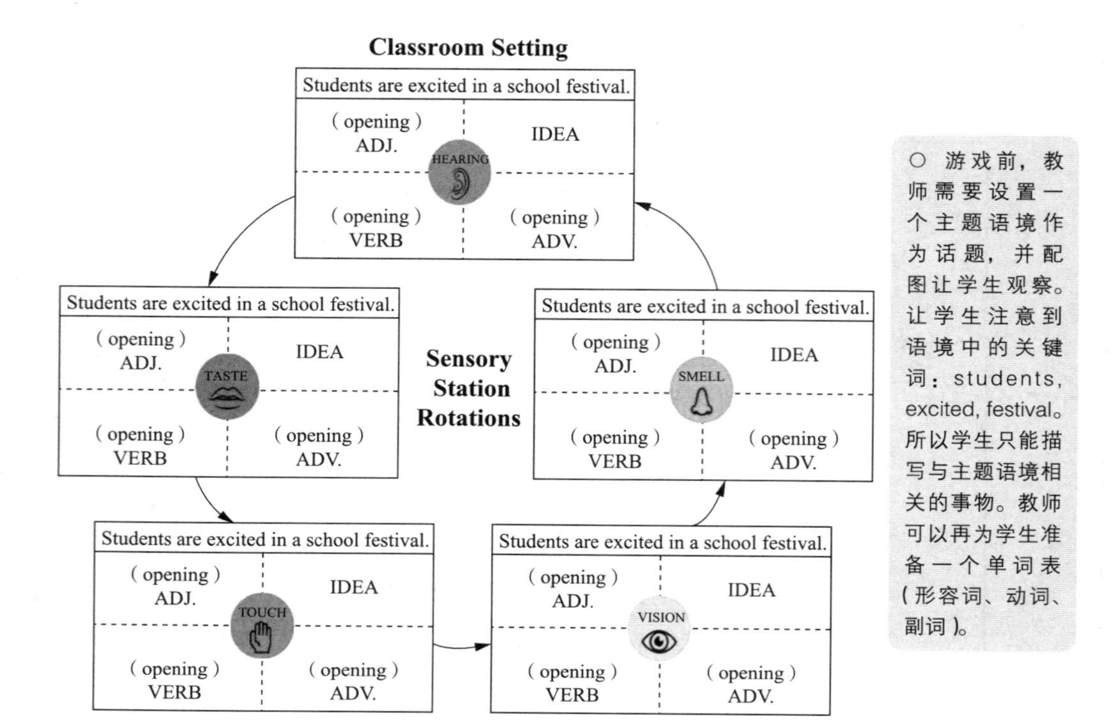

○ 游戏前，教师需要设置一个主题语境作为话题，并配图让学生观察。让学生注意到语境中的关键词：students, excited, festival。所以学生只能描写与主题语境相关的事物。教师可以再为学生准备一个单词表（形容词、动词、副词）。

- Explain to students that they will brainstorm all sensory details for one scene: *Students are excited in a school festival.* They can choose relevant adjectives, adverbs or verbs from the word bank to describe the idea. The teacher must demonstrate how to work on each station. Students are free to write words or draw line image on the poster. See how to brainstorm on each station:

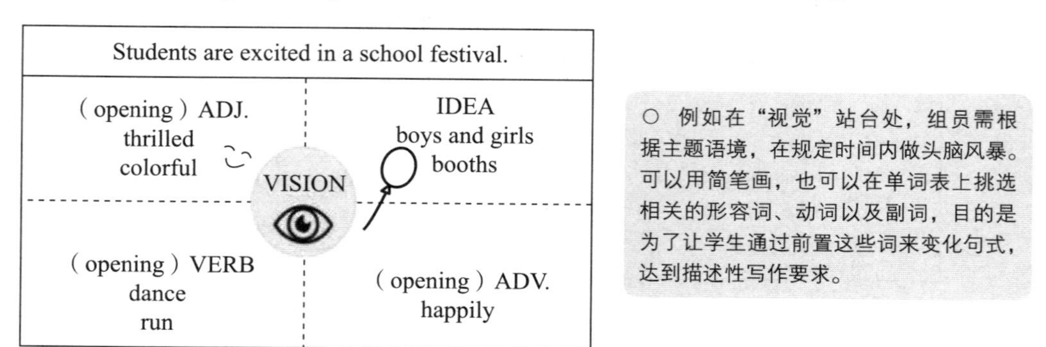

○ 例如在“视觉”站台处，组员需根据主题语境，在规定时间内做头脑风暴。可以用简笔画，也可以在单词表上挑选相关的形容词、动词以及副词，目的是为了让学生通过前置这些词来变化句式，达到描述性写作要求。

- Each group has 2 minutes to work on each station. Cue each group to rotate (clockwise or anti-clockwise) to the next station by playing another song.

When hearing the change of a song, each group should put down the marker pen and quickly run to the next station. Each group will have opportunities to brainstorm all 5 sensory stations.

- When rotation finishes, each group should stay where they begin from. Make one "showing" sentence by combing the information on the station. Answers may vary:

○ 在游戏结束后，教师可以让每组学生按照站台上的信息，用前置句式造句并简要地给出评价。

Thrilled, boys and girls run from one vendor booth to another.

Happily, colorful balloons dance with boys and girls in the school party.

Joining the school party, colorful balloons dance above the booths.

Encourage weaker students to come up with simple showing sentences such as:

Colorful balloons dance happily in the school.

Happy students run on the playground.

- Distribute the worksheets of Graphic Organizer. Lead students through each part of Graphic Organizer (telling and showing). Have students write the telling part individually. They can look or walk around to search the information they need from 5 stations. See Graphic Organizer and possible answers:

Graphic Organizer		
Scene: Students are excited in a school festival		
Telling	Vision	I can see students, booths and balloons.
	Hearing	I can hear music, laughter and screams.
	Smell	
	Taste	
	Touch	I can feel the heat.
Showing	Thrilled, boys and girls move from one vendor booth to another. Joining the party, balloons dance above booths, with a June sun rising from behind. The ice cream vendor has a heyday. Everyone shouts over the heads of others and fights to get ice cream, taking them straight to their mouths. There is also a rush at the barbeque vendor, dominated by grilled chicken wings, sausages, fish and chips. Funny music drifts into ears along with the screams and laughter.	

○ 教师可以让学生在课堂内完成"telling"部分的写作任务。根据不同程度，选取2～4个感官进行描写。提示学生在showing部分中，尽量避免出现"I can see"，"I can hear"等"telling"句式。这也是此游戏的教学目的。

WORD BANK
BE MORE DESCRIPTIVE!

Adjectives	Verb	Adverb
■ Buttery	• Drift	◆ Briskly
■ Cheesy	• Fly	◆ Openly
■ Fantastic	• Cheer	◆ Urgently
■ Amused	• Laugh	◆ Optimistically
■ Cheerful	• Chuckle	◆ Tremendously
■ Loud	• Giggle	◆ Youthfully
■ Warm	• Roar	◆ Restfully
■ Dry	• Run	◆ Lively
■ Smooth	• Race	◆ Closely
■ Cold	• Dash	◆ Loudly
■ Charmed	• Rush	◆ Continually
■ Cheerful	• Jog	◆ Gently
■ Contented	• Jump	◆ Lovingly
■ Delighted	• Bounce	◆ Coolly
■ Ecstatic	• Bound	◆ Nicely
■ Creamy	• Buzz	◆ Beautifully
■ Grilled	• Boom	◆ Surprisingly

○ 教师也可以加大难度，混合一些不相关的词语，学生则需根据不同主题语境选择相关的词语。

该游戏叫做“五感循环”，旨在帮助学生运用“五感法”进行描写。在描述性写作中，学生往往缺乏对细节的观察以及合适的语言措辞，例如：描写要素与想表达的主题无关，随意性较大；描写无法让读者“可视化”；描述语竭词穷，以“I see”，“I hear”的“telling”句子居多。所以可以通过把形容词、动词、副词（或词组）前置来帮助学生在语言上从“telling”过渡到“showing”。

学生通过在五个感官站台中轮换，切身感受到可以通过不同感官来描写相同的场景，表达同一种情绪或是主题，丰富写作内容，也能让读者“可视化”，使文章更生动。通过该游戏能让学生理解描述性写作的特点，也能更好地理解“Show, don’t tell”的写作要领。

79 Creating Codes

Focus: Text-Coding

Level: All Levels

Duration: 15~20 minutes

Procedure:

- Distribute worksheets to students. Working in pairs or groups, students will need to match these codes to the meaning and share within the class.

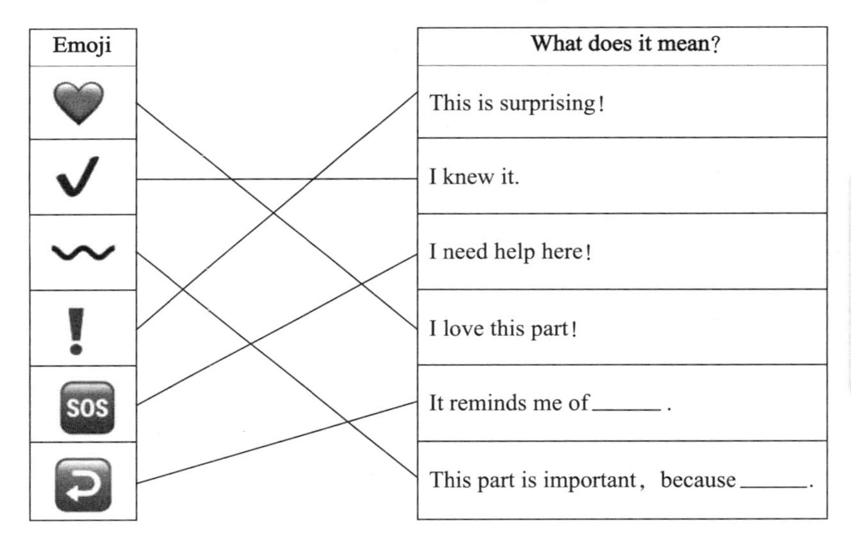

○ 在符号的选择上老师可以有自己的创意，或是和学生一起创造出一套代码系统便于之后的课堂使用。

- The teacher will have to model how to implement these symbols to code a text. Read a story to the whole class and pause to demonstrate each symbol. After the demonstration ask students to try by themselves and share with each other in groups. Text-coding can be applied to any genre and teachers can use it as an interactive-reading strategy while students can always use it as a way to annotate the text. See a sample from a novel:

○ 建议教师选择一个简短有趣的故事作为示范。可以把符号都打印在 A4 纸上。教师边读边在需要停顿处示意学生如何使用符号。

An extract from *The Adventures of Tom Sawyer*

Tom and Becky walked down a winding passage[1] inside a cave, holding their candles high. They saw names and dates written on the wall with candle smoke by other visitors to the cave. Becky and Tom read some of them as they walked along. They were talking so much that it was a little while before they noticed they were now in a part of the cave that had no writing on the wall. They used candle smoke to write their own names on the rock and walked on.

Soon they came to a place where a little stream of water was running. Over the years the cave wall had been shaped by the running stream, and it looked like a frozen waterfall. Tom went behind it and lit it up with his candle so that Becky could see it better. Behind the stone waterfall he found an opening in the rock, leading downwards. At once he wanted to explore it. Becky agreed and together they started to walk down into the earth. They wound this way and that, far into the cave, making smoke marks here and there to show the way back. This was exciting. They would have a lot to tell their friends above when they returned.

In one place, they found a huge, open space full of shining stalactites[2], as long and thick as a man's leg. They walked around it and left by one of the many passages that opened into it. The next place they found was full of bats. There were thousands of them. The candlelight woke them up, and they flew at the candle flames at once. Tom knew this was dangerous and took Becky's hand to hurry her away. He pulled her into the first opening he found. And none too soon, one of the bats put out Becky's candle with its wings as she ran away. The bats chased them quite a long way, but Tom and Becky ran into every new passage that they came to, and at last they got away.

内容来源：《牛津英语（上海版）》九年级下册第五单元 More Practice：An extract from *The Adventures of Tom Sawyer*

See a sample from an informational text:

Scientist discovers a sixth sense

As we all know, there are five senses: hearing, smell, sight, taste and touch. Now, however, a scientist has shown that we have a sixth sense: the ability① to know when someone is watching us. *Surprising!*

Many people have noticed this feeling. For example, you are sitting in a cinema, and you feel that someone is watching you. You look around quickly, and find that you are right. A friend, at the back of the cinema, is staring at you. *I often feel that way too.*

Until now, no one has been able to prove scientifically that people really do have this ability. But recently a scientist called Dr Rupert Sheldrake has announced the results of some new experiments. *It has been proved!*

The experiments work in this way. Imagine② two girls, Emma and Claire. Emma sits on a chair and wears a blindfold over her eyes, so she cannot see. Claire sits a few metres behind Emma. A teacher blows a whistle③. Then in random④ order, Claire either looks at Emma, or she looks in a different direction. Emma must say whether Claire is looking at her or not. The experiment is repeated 20 times. *Will try it!*

Dr Sheldrake repeated this simple experiment with hundreds of children. The results were that the person who was wearing the blindfold, like Emma, could often feel that the other person was watching him or her. Generally, the children knew about 60% of the time they were being watched. If the children were just guessing 'yes' or 'no', the result would only be 50%. *Strong evidence!*

Some scientists say they do not agree that there is a sixth sense. They say it is impossible to feel something in this way. But Dr Sheldrake says that the results are accurate. 'These experiments were carried out by different people in different countries,' he said, 'and yet they all showed almost the same results.' *Still Controversial! SOS Define "different": age? nationality? gender?*

内容来源：《牛津英语（上海版）》八年级下册第五单元 More Practice：Scientists discovers a sixth sense

这个游戏叫做“创造代码”，通过运用各种符号帮助学生解析语篇。“代码”没有统一的标准，但需要简单、清晰、便于学生操作，其目的是帮助学生在阅读时勤加思考、追踪想法并记录下来。这些信息有助于学生解读语篇、展开课堂讨论。

该游戏能帮助教师在阅读课中有效地与学生展开互动，且适用于各类型文本。在案例中可以看到，学生记录下了当时的一些想法，可以是对情节的理解、评论、困惑，也可以是对过往亲身经历的联想。这些想法无关乎对错，是当下真实反应的体现。教师在课堂中可以就这些想法组织小组讨论、分享感悟以及点评总结，以此增加阅读课的互动性。该游戏更重要的目的是培养学生在自主阅读时思考问题以及做笔记的习惯。

建议教师在带领全班操练几次后让学生自主进行练习。按照实际需求，可以用这个活动让学生预习文本，也可以在分析文本前当作一个互动讨论环节。

80 Shrinking

Focus: Summarizing Informational Texts

Level: Advanced

Duration: 20～30 minutes

Procedure:

- Before the game, explain to students that summary writing focuses students' attention on main ideas, which encourages students to read and write purposefully.
- Provide each student with a picture. Ask them what their dominant impression is and think about how to summarize what they see in this picture objectively. See the sample picture below:

- Ask students to segment the picture according to the order of description. And in each segment, circle out one item that stands out to them (avoid repetition). Illustrate the item on the margin. See the sample response below:

○ 建议教师选择主题较为明确，并包含人或物的图片。根据以下步骤开展活动：

1. 确定描写顺序，分割图片。
2. 学生在描述每块小图片时，只选取一个重点进行描述，并将内容写在空白处。
3. 用挑选的词语造句。（一句即可）
4. 把四句结合成段。

- Students write one sentence by using the words on the margin for each segment. Combine the sentences into one paragraph and share it with the partner.

○ 游戏之后，可以让学生自己讨论 summary 的特点。待学生理解之后再开始阅读写作训练。

- Tell students that the concept of summary is "shrinking" a large amount of information by focusing on a key point.
- After the game, have students work in small groups to read an informational text. Tell them to summarize the whole text by applying the "shrinking" method.
- Working in a group of 4, students read the text with the leading of the teacher. Ask students to stop after each paragraph, underline one sentence that stands

out to them. And then in that sentence, circle out one word or phrase that stands out to them and put this word in the margin. See the sample text and response.

Review by Tony Ma

This book says our world is in danger. It describes the various threats to the environment. The situation is so serious that we must do something to save the Earth.

The greenhouse effect

The writers ask us to 'imagine that the Earth is inside a kind of greenhouse with the atmosphere around it. The atmosphere acts like the glass: it lets sunlight in and keeps warmth from getting out. The atmosphere is essential for all living things. Without it, the Earth would be as cold and lifeless as the surface of the moon'.

'The trouble is that our atmosphere is changing because we are polluting it with chemicals—in the form of gases—and it is keeping in too much heat!'

These gases, mainly carbon dioxide (CO_2), are produced by burning fuels such as petrol. The greenhouse effect may cause the level of the sea to rise and flood cities and even whole countries.

Damage to the ozone layer

The writers tell us that ozone is a gas which occurs 20 to 50 km above the ground. It forms an essential protective layer around the Earth. Without it, the Sun would burn us up'.

We are making holes in the ozone layer, mainly by using chemicals called CFCs. We use these in fridges and spray cans, and to make plastic items such as fast food boxes.

Destruction of the forests

The burning and cutting down of the forests is making the greenhouse effect worse because trees take in CO_2. It also causes soil erosion and flooding, as well as destroying the homes of people and animals that live in the forests.

Bad habits

Many of our habits cause pollution, especially our habit of using things once and then throwing them away. This creates massive mountains of rubbish. We do not know what to do with the rubbish and it pollutes our land and sea. For example, people throw away as many as seven billion drink cans in Britain each year. That is enough to reach from the Earth to the moon.

How can we save the Earth?

The book is asking us to become 'green consumers'. That means we should only buy and use environmentally friendly goods so that we can save the Earth. These goods will not damage the environment.

Let's be green consumers and enjoy living a better life on the Earth!

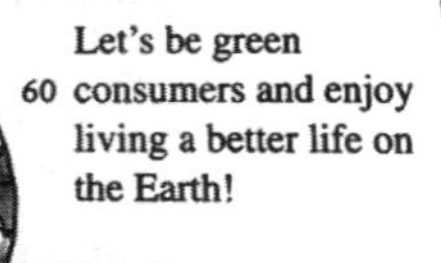

○ 按照文章的段落，从每个段落找出一句关键句，再圈出一个关键词写在空白处。告诉学生用关键词写一个句子即可。

（内容来源：《牛津英语（上海版）》九年级下册 Unit 1 Saving the earth）

- Distribute worksheets for students to review the criteria before start summarizing. See the sample worksheets:

Summary	Summary Criteria Tick if he/she has it.
1. ____ 2. ____ 3. ____ 4. ____ 5. ____ 6. ____ 7. ____ 8. ____ 9. ____ 10. ____	• Is shorter than the original text. • Incorporates main ideas and excludes details. • Is written in the order information appears in the original text. • Does not include the opinion of the writer.

See the sample response:

(1) The Earth functions like a greenhouse with atmosphere.

(2) People are polluting the atmosphere with gases.

(3) It is fuels that produce gases.

(4) Ozone is also a gas to protect the Earth.

(5) People are making holes in the Ozone layer.

(6) The greenhouse effect gets worse because of destruction of the forests.

(7) Bad habits produce rubbish.

(8) We need to work collaboratively to save the Earth.

○ 用关键词造完句之后，再将句子合并成段。需提醒学生注意逻辑关系，需使用连接词并再加以润色修改。

- Use criteria for self-check and peer-check in the group. Share in the class with teacher's feedback.

这个游戏叫做“缩水”，旨在指导学生如何缩减不必要的信息并保留关键信息来总结说明文。教师可根据学生程度及语篇难度，带领学生一起完成，或给学生示范几段之后，让学生自主完成剩余部分。若文章较难，段落较少，教师可以帮助学生继续分段帮助理解。在动笔写之前，需要让学生了解“何为有效的总结？”“有效的总结有哪些标准？”。

待学生连句成段后，教师需让学生对比原文，让学生检查是否只保留了关键信息。教师可以展示及点评多个学生的总结，鼓励学生相互学习、发现问题并予以修正。

Part Five

Language Function
（语言功能）

81 Would You Mind...?

Focus: Asking for, Giving and Refusing Permission

Level: Elementary

Duration: 5～10 minutes

Procedure:

- Tell the students that they are going to ask for, give and refuse permission, using the cards as prompts.
- Give each student one "asking for permission" card and one "giving permission" card. The two cards don't match with each other.
- The students move around, asking different students at random for permission to do something, using the prompts on their "asking for permission" card. Students' responses depend on whether they have the corresponding "giving permission" card. If they do not have the corresponding card, they refuse. If they do have the corresponding card, they agree and give the card to the person who asks. The game continues until every student has two corresponding cards (one "asking for permission" card and one corresponding "giving permission" card).

○ 学生不能互看对方卡片以及随意交换卡片，他们必须运用语言来表达手中"征求许可卡"上的内容，只有对方同意时，方可获得对方的"准许卡"。而被征求的一方，要根据征求者的语言和自己是否有相应的"准许卡"作出同意或拒绝的回应。

Examples:

Sample of the cards:

	Asking for permission: **turn on the radio**

	Giving permission: **turn on the radio**

○ 卡片有两种类型，分别是“征求许可卡”和“准许卡”，每张“征求许可卡”上都有不同的征求许可内容，且都有一张与之相对应的“准许卡”。

Sample dialogue:

Student A: Would you mind if I turn on the radio?

Students B: I'm sorry, I'm afraid I do mind.

Student A: Would you mind if I turn on the radio?

Students C: No, of course not.

这个游戏名为“你介不介意……？”，这是一个卡片配对游戏，旨在帮助学生熟练运用恰当的语言来征求许可和回应许可，以达到交际目的。游戏伊始，每位学生都有一张“征求许可卡”和与之无关的一张“准许卡”。游戏规定每位同学都要从其他人那里获取与自己手中“征求许可卡”相匹配的“准许卡”，其方式是要向不同的人表达出自己手中“征求许可卡”上的内容，直到对方有匹配的“准许卡”并且以语言回应表示同意时，方可获得这张“准许卡”。

征求许可的表达方式有很多，有正式和非正式的，取决于对话双方的关系。所以，教师可以在游戏之前为学生设定合适的语境，而学生则要在既定的语境下，运用恰当的语言征求对方许可，比如向熟悉的朋友征求许可，可以用 *Can I...?* 向不熟悉的人或者尊者征求许可，那么用 *Would you mind...?* 会更正式、更有礼貌。通过这样设定情境的方式，学生能更进一步明确如何选择适切的语言来征求他人许可。

82 Will It Happen?

Focus: Expressing Certainty and Uncertainty

Level: Elementary

Duration: 10～15 minutes

Procedure:

- Set the context by telling the students that they are going to ask and answer questions about their future.
- Give each student a worksheet. Ask them to read through the questions on the worksheet and create two more questions of their own at the end.
- In pairs, the students ask their partner the questions on their worksheet and record their partner's answers by ticking in the corresponding column. They also ask follow-up questions to gain more information.

○ 教师要鼓励学生不要仅停留于任务单上的问题，可以适当延伸，问一些后续问题，如 Why are you so sure？ What language will you learn？等。

Examples:

Sample worksheet:

Do you think you will..?	I'm sure I will	I probably will	I might	I probably won't	I definitely won't
do some exercise after school					
drink some coffee today					
pass the exam tomorrow					
go to the cinema this week					
get up early this weekend					
make a new friend in the next few days					
travel abroad this year					
learn a new language in the next five years					
win a lottery in the next ten years					
become famous in your life					
...					

○ 任务单上的问题主要是围绕学生日常活动的话题，让学生谈论自己的未来。教师也可以改变话题，由谈论他们自己的未来变成谈论人类的未来等。最后，适当的留白给学生提供自由发挥的空间，让他们自己设置问题，使交流更真实。

Sample dialogue:

Student A: Do you think you will pass the exam tomorrow?

Student B: Yes, I'm sure I will. How about you?

Student A: I probably won't. I think it is hard to pass the exam. Why are you so sure about it?

Student B: Why not? I have prepared everything well for the exam.

这个游戏名为“这会发生吗？”。通过这个游戏可以帮助学生熟练运用恰当的语言来表达对自己未来的确定与不确定，达到交际目的。游戏开始前，教师要教授学生一些用于表达确定与不确定的语言，如用 sure、definitely 来描述确定的事，用 probably、might 来描述存疑的事，且 might 表达的可能性比 probably 更低。游戏以两人为一组完成，互相询问对方对自己未来的想法，话题围绕学生日常生活展开，因此，学生只需要按照自身实际来谈论即可。这个游戏适合基础层次的学生，它为学生搭建了语言支架，学生只需要运用教师设定的问题和刚学过的语言知识来进行问答，学生通过反复操练句型加深印象，学会如何表达确定与不确定，除此之外，还能进一步复习巩固一般将来时和相关的时间状语。

这个游戏也可以用于自由练习，学生有一定的自由度，比如，他们可以自由表达自己对未来的看法，也可以自己设置想问的问题，还可以在对话过程中，根据对方的回答提出后续问题，获取更多的信息，增进同学之间的了解。

83 Good News, Bad News

Focus: Delivering Good News and Bad News

Level: Lower-intermediate

Duration: 15～20 minutes

Procedure:

- Divide the class into groups of 4. Give each group a game board, a coin and a set of cards. Ask the students to shuffle the cards, place them face down in the middle of the board, choose a small thing (e.g. a rubber) as their own counter and put their counters on the four corners of the board.

- The students take turns to toss the coin and move their own counter along the board accordingly (1 step for head and 2 steps for tail). When they land on a square with a speech bubble, they pick a card, deliver the news on the card to the student on their right and make a dialogue. The first student to get back to his/her starting corner wins the game.

○ 在游戏开始前，教师需要让学生明确掷硬币的规则，如掷到正面表示可在棋盘上向前进一步，掷到反面则表示向前进两步。同时，教师也要鼓励学生在游戏过程中将自身带入到卡片所提供的情境中去，以角色身份向他人传达信息，尽可能还原真实的生活场景。

- Invite several students to perform how they deliver the news and ask other students to evaluate the way they deliver the news. Then help the students to summarize some tips on how to deliver good news and bad news.

Examples:

Sample of the game board:

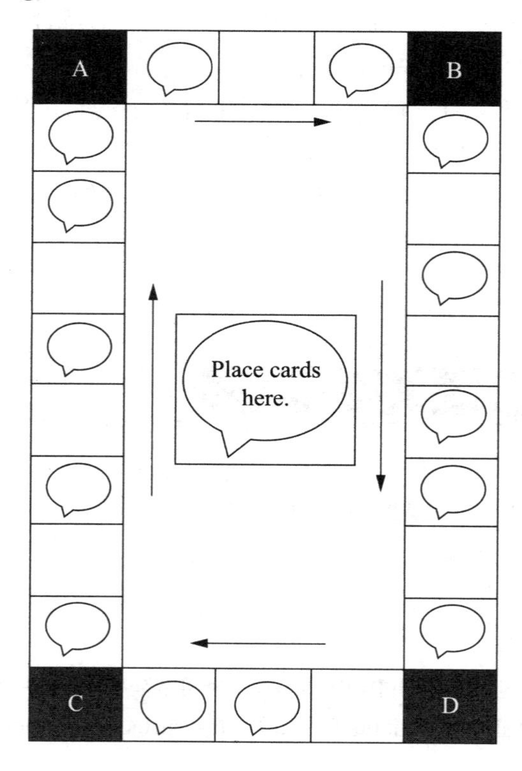

Sample cards:

You are a student. Tell your classmate he/she didn't pass the exam.	You are a vet. Tell the pet owner his/her pet was dead.
You are a student. Tell your friend you can't go to his/her birthday party.	You are a student. Tell your neighbour you broke his/her window.
You are a child. Tell your parent you spoiled some cola on his/her phone and it stopped working.	You are a parent. Tell your child you won't be able to take him/her to the amusement park this weekend.
You are an interviewer. Tell your interviewee he/she doesn't get the job.	You are a doctor. Tell your patient he/she has got a serious disease.
You are a teacher. Tell your classmate he/she got the first prize in the contest.	You are a student. Tell your friend you will give him/her two free tickets to a concert.
You are a boss. Tell your employee you have agreed to raise his/her salary.	You are a parent. Tell your child you will buy him/her a new bicycle.
You are a manager. Tell your customer he/she won the jackpot this week.	You are a doctor. Tell your patient he/she was completely cured.

○ 教师在制作卡片时，要选择简练的语言，让学生一目了然，能明确自己是何身份、要传递信息的对象是谁，以及要传递的信息是什么。

Sample dialogue:

Student A: Emily, I've got some bad news. I'm afraid that I won't be able to take you to the amusement park this weekend.

Student B: Why? You promised me and we've already bought the tickets.

Student A: Yes..., but I have to work, so I won't be able to go with you. I know it really sucks and I'm really sorry to let you down. What about going there next time?

Student B: Fine.

这个游戏名为“好消息，坏消息”，这是一个棋盘游戏，能帮助学生熟练运用恰当的语言来向他人传达好消息与坏消息。这个游戏的关键在于它为学生提供了许多真实的情境，为他们设定了不同的角色身份，有他们原本的学生身份，也有他们熟悉的家长、教师、医生等身份。他们要根据设定的情境和身份来进行对话，完成信息的传达，实现真实的交际。

教师借此游戏不仅可以帮助学生复习巩固那些用于传达消息的交际用语，还可以借此教学生一些沟通技巧，尤其是在日常生活中如何正确地向他人传达坏消息。比如，在传达坏消息时，需根据自身与对方的关系，谨慎地选择措辞，用委婉、哀伤或懊悔的语气陈述事实，还要时刻留意对方的情绪变化，根据不同的情况，及时地表达安慰、提供帮助、表示歉意或解释缘由等，尽可能缓解对方的负面情绪。

84 Let's Go Together!

Focus: Making, Accepting and Declining an Invitation

Level: Lower-intermediate and above

Duration: 10～15 minutes

Procedure:

- Set the context by telling the students that they are going to invite someone out this weekend.

- Hand out the cards, one for each student. Give the students 30 seconds to read the card and ask if there are any words they do not know on the card.
- The students move around, inviting their classmates to go to the place on their card. They can invite as many classmates as they wish. Every time someone accepts, they write down his or her name and the appointed time on the card. Everyone is free to accept or decline the invitations.

○ 学生自行决定接受或拒绝他人的邀请，但是接受邀请的同学要与对方约定时间，而拒绝邀请的同学也要给出相应的理由。

- Stop the game when you feel the students have had enough practice. The person who invites the most classmates wins the game.

Examples:

Sample card:

Taco Bell

Best Mexican food in town

Open Time: 10 a.m.-10 p.m.

Name: ________ Time: ________

Name: ________ Time: ________

Name: ________ Time: ________

Name: ________ Time: ________

○ 卡片分为上下两个部分。卡片的上半部分提供了休闲娱乐场所的信息，如场所名字、主营内容和营业时间等。学生可根据卡片上的信息向其他同学发起邀约。卡片的下半部分供学生记录接受邀请的人以及约定的时间。

Sample dialogue:

Student A: Do you like Mexican food?

Student B: Yes, I do.

Student A: Great. Would you like to go to Taco Bell with me this weekend?

Student B: Sure. What time?

Student A: How about 6 o' clock on Saturday evening?

Student B: Sounds fine. See you then.

这个游戏名为“我们一起去吧！”，旨在训练学生运用恰当的语言来发出邀请和回应邀请，达到交际目的。学生要根据手中卡片的信息，向其他同学发起邀请，邀请他们在周末共同前往卡片上的地方。对于他人的邀请，学生可以欣然接受，并进一步询问信息；也可以礼貌拒绝，并给出合理的理由。最后，邀请成功次数最多的人为游戏的获胜者。这样的游戏设定大大地激发了学生开口表达的欲望，让学生在不知不觉中反复训练用于表达邀请和回应邀请的交际用语。

卡片是该游戏的重要道具，教师需根据学生的数量，预先准备好足够数量的卡片。教师制作卡片时可以选择各式各样的场所进行介绍，如餐馆、电影院、博物馆、运动场馆等，为学生提供丰富的语言材料；或者，也可以让学生自己制作卡片，选择自己最爱去的场所进行介绍，以增加游戏的趣味性和学生的参与度。

85 Who Is Who?

Focus: Describing People

Level: Lower-intermediate and above

Duration: 10～15 minutes

Procedure:

- Tell the students that they are going to play a guessing game in which they need to describe the people on the sheet and guess who others are describing.
- Elicit the vocabulary from the students, which they could use to describe people. Then write the related vocabulary on the blackboard.
- Divide the students into groups of 3 or 4. Give each group two copies of the character sheet. Ask them to put one sheet face up on the table for group members to see, cut the other one into separate cards, and then put them in a pile face down in the middle.

○ 每组会拿到两张一样的印有人物图片的纸，一张无需裁剪，正面朝上摆放在桌上；另一张则将纸裁开，变成一张张人物卡片，正面朝下堆放在桌上。教师也可提前裁剪好人物卡片。

- The students take turns to take a card without showing it to others and describe the person on it. The rest of the students in the group raise questions and guess who is being described. The card is given to the first one who gets the right answer. If someone gets the wrong answer, put the card back on the bottom of the pile. The game continues until there's no card left in the middle. The student with the most cards is the winner.

○ 教师要提醒学生，在一位同学描述卡片上的人物时，其他同学进行提问并猜测，猜测的机会只有一次，需要抢答，第一位猜并猜中的同学可以获得这张卡片。一旦猜错，就要将卡片重新放回，等下次这张卡片被描述时再进行猜测。这意味着学生既要猜得快，又要猜得准。

Examples:

Sample of the character sheet:

○ 教师可以增减人物的数量，以控制游戏时长。在选择人物时，应选择一些具有不同外貌特征的人物，也可以穿插几个外貌相似的人物来增加游戏难度。建议图片最好用彩色打印，以便学生描述。

Sample of related vocabulary:

Height	short, average height, tall
Build	well-built, slim, plump, petite
Age	elderly, middle-aged, young
Colouring	fair, white, blonde, dark
Face	round, oval, heart-shaped, square
Hair	bald, straight, curly, wavy
Clothes	suit, shirt, dress, shoes
Accessories	belt, glasses, watch, hat
Other features	beard, moustache, a hooked nose, dimples

Sample dialogue:

Student A: Is he a male?

Student B: Yes, he is.

Student C: What does he look like?

Student B: He is bald. He is tall and thin. He has green eyes. He has a black beard and a moustache.

Student A: Is he Luke?

Student B: Yes.

这个游戏名为“谁是谁？”，这是一个竞猜游戏，旨在帮助学生练习运用恰当的语言来询问及描述人物的特征，如长相、身材、衣着等，达到交际目的。游戏以三人或四人为一组，每位学生轮流抽取一张卡片并描述卡片上人物的特征，而其他同学根据其描述进行提问与竞猜。

这个游戏能很好地兼顾趣味性与有效性，趣味性在于它能激发学生的竞争意识，他们一起比赛谁能更快速、更准确地猜中被描述的人物；有效性在于它能使学生聚焦于人物特征，一方面是学生要自己口头描述人物特征，另一方面则是要听别人描述人物特征，学生在听与说的过程中进一步巩固用于描述人物特征的语言。

另外，教师也可以借此游戏培养学生的跨文化意识，告诉学生在描述人物特征时要注意措辞。例如，在形容一个人胖的时候，不能用 fat，因为这个词带有强烈的贬义，可以选择一些更委婉的词来表达，比如用 chubby 形容小孩子胖嘟嘟、用 plump 形容女性丰满、用 big-boned 形容男性块头大，等等。

86 Do You Like It?

Focus: Talking About Likes and Dislikes

Level: Lower-intermediate and above

Duration: 15～20 minutes

Procedure:

- Divide the students into groups of 2～4 and explain the rules of the game.
- Give each group a game board and a dice. Ask each student to choose a small thing (e.g. a rubber) as their counter. Tell them to put the game board in the middle of the table and put their counters on the START square.
- Everyone in the group rolls the dice. The student with the largest number on the dice starts the game. The students take turns to roll the dice and move their counter along the board accordingly. When a student lands on a square, he/she talks about the topic on the square for 30 seconds, expressing how much he/she likes or dislikes it. If a student has nothing to say on the topic or speaks for less than 30 seconds, the rest of the students in the group ask him/her several follow-up questions. The first student to land on the FINISH square wins the game.

○ 在游戏开始前，教师可以教授学生一些游戏用语，如“It's your turn.”“Roll the dice.”“Move your counter.”等，学生可用于在游戏中进行交流。

Examples:

Sample of the game board:

FINISH		swimming	winter	learning English	reality shows
getting up early		Go forward one space			shopping
soft drinks		doing housework		Super skip! Go forward	fast food
the place you live		school life		travelling	
Go back two spaces		computer games		coffee	
family members		sweet food		weekends	
horror movies		reading books		snakes	
rainy days		Oh no! Go back		sports	music
Miss a turn	pop stars	durian			START

○ 棋盘上的话题是学生在游戏中要进行讨论的，因此，教师应尽量选择一些学生比较熟悉的、有话可说的话题。

Sample dialogue:

Student A: I like music very much. My favourite thing to do at the end of a long day is to listen to music. It can always help soothe my nerves and put me in a better mood.

Student B: What kind of music are you into?

Student A: I'm a big fan of classical music.

Student B: Why do you like classical music?

Student A: Unlike other types of music, classical music has been popular for a long time. It is more inspiring and enjoyable.

这个游戏名为“你喜不喜欢？”，这是一个棋盘游戏，可以帮助学生巩固表示喜欢与不喜欢的句型，使学生能够运用恰当的语言来表达个人偏好，达到交际目的。在游戏过程中，学生用学过的句型表达对某个人、某件事或某样东西的喜好程度，可以是喜欢，可以是讨厌，也可以是既不喜欢也不讨厌，这取决于学生自己。为了鼓励学生表达，游戏规定每个人在表达好恶时都要说满 30 秒，若某位学生无话可说时，组内的其他同学可以继续向其提问，如“Why do you like it?”“How often do you do it?”等，既让这位学生有话可说，也可提高其他学生的专注力与参与度。

87 Compliment Bag

Focus: Giving and Responding to Compliments

Level: Lower-intermediate and above

Duration: 15～20 minutes

Procedure:

- Ask the students to brainstorm the words and expressions that can be used to give and respond to compliments. Then, provide them with the word list and expression list for reference if necessary.
- Make two name cards for each student. Mix all the cards together and put them into a compliment bag.
- Demonstrate how to play the game by picking a name card from the bag, giving a compliment to the student on the name card and then passing the bag to that student.
- The student who receives a compliment responds to the compliment and continues the game by repeating what the teacher does.

○ 在游戏开始前，教师可以提醒学生在赞美他人时要注意的事项，如：第一，赞美要真实，赞美的内容要符合赞美的对象；第二，赞美要具体，避免用过于笼统的词，尽量用具体的词和具体的事例；第三，赞美时要注意眼神交流，要面带微笑，语气真诚。

Any student who gets his/her own name card should put it back and pick a new one. The game continues until there is no name card left in the bag.

Examples:

Sample word list:

Word list		
artistic	easygoing	intelligent
athletic	energetic	kind
brave	enthusiastic	motivated
calm	faithful	open-minded
careful	friendly	optimistic
caring	generous	reliable
charming	gentle	responsible
cheerful	gorgeous	selfless
clever	handsome	sincere
confident	helpful	smart
considerate	honest	sociable
creative	humble	talented
delightful	humorous	thoughtful
determined	imaginative	wise
diligent	insightful	witty

○ 教师可以根据学生的能力水平来决定词汇表上的单词，帮助学生用更为丰富、更具体的词来赞美他人。

Sample expression list:

Expression list
Giving compliments: You are so.../ You are such a... You are really good at... You did a good job at.../ You really did well in... I like.../ I love... I appreciate... Thank you for... I've never met someone... It was nice of you to... **Responding to compliments:** Thanks./ Thank you./ Thank you for saying that. That means a lot to me. You're so sweet. I appreciate that. I needed to hear that. I'm happy to hear you feel that way. Do you really think so? I don't think so, but thanks for saying so.

Sample dialogue:

Student A: I've never met someone as kind as you are. You are such a good listener. You are my favorite person to talk to.

Student B: Thank you. I'm happy to hear you feel that way.

这个游戏名为“赞美袋”。通过这个游戏能帮助学生练习运用恰当的语言来赞美他人，如赞美他人的外貌、性格、才能等，同时，运用恰当的语言来回应他人的赞美，达到交际目的。赞美是非常重要的一项人际交往技巧，能有效地拉近人与人之间的距离。不同于外国人比较善于表达自己的心情和想法，中国人大多数是比较含蓄的，在现实生活中有许多人不善于赞美他人，也不习惯接受来自他人的赞美，因而生活中缺少了很多愉快的情绪体验。这个游戏能促使学生去发现身边人的优点，鼓励他们用真诚的语言去表达，也让他们有机会听到来自身边人的肯定，增强自我认同感。

88 Ring! Ring! Ring!

Focus: Making and Receiving Phone Calls

Level: Intermediate

Duration: 10～15 minutes

Procedure:

- Divide the students into groups of 4. Give each group a set of A cards and B cards.
- The students shuffle the cards together and deal them out evenly. They then read the cards in their hands. Any student who already has an A card and the corresponding B card can directly read them aloud to the group, e.g. "Who's calling, please?" "My name is Mathew Smith." If all the students in the group agree that the two cards go together, the owner can lay the two cards down face up on the table.
- The students take turns to read an A card to

○ 在游戏过程中，学生不能给别人看自己手中卡片上的内容，只能读给别人听。因此，学生要清晰地说出卡片上的内容，同时还要仔细听别人说，理解说话人要表达的意思。

the other students in their group. The student who has the corresponding B card reads it aloud to the group. If all the students in the group agree that the two cards can go together, the two cards are then placed face up on the table. The game continues until all the students have no more cards in their hands. The first group with the most pairs of matching cards is the winner.

Examples:

Sample cards:

A	B
A Who's calling, please?	**B** My name is Mathew Smith.
A Hello, may I speak to Paul, please?	**B** Yes, speaking.
A The line is terrible. You are breaking up.	**B** OK. I'll call you back on another line.
A I'm sorry, Maggie is out of the office today.	**B** I see. Could I leave a message for her, please?
A Do you know when she will be back?	**B** She will be back at three o'clock.
A Could you spell that for me, please?	**B** OK. It's G-A-T-I-S-S.
A I'm afraid he isn't in right now. Can I take a message?	**B** Yes, please. Could you ask him to call me back?
A Can you hold on a second, please?	**B** OK, I'll wait.
A Can I have your phone number?	**B** It's 8877-6256.
A Hello, this is Ross Geller. I'm calling for Andrew Scott. Is he available?	**B** I'm afraid he is busy at the moment.

○ 游戏卡片有A、B两种，每张卡片上都印有一些打电话时常用到的话语。每张A卡都有一张与之对应的B卡，上面的内容恰好是对话时的一问一答。卡片的总数应是每组组员数的倍数，以确保游戏初始时每位玩家拥有的卡片数是相同的。教师可以根据学生水平或教学目标调整卡片上的内容和卡片数量。

续表

A	B
A Let me just repeat that back to you. Your e-mail is Mike123@mail.com.	**B** Yes, that's right.
A There is no one here by that name. I think you've got the wrong number.	**B** Oh, sorry for troubling you.
A I didn't catch that. Could you say that again?	**B** Yes, I said could you tell him that I'll arrive at five o'clock instead of six.
A I'll pass your message on as soon as he's free.	**B** Thank you.
A I phoned a moment ago, but I was cut off.	**B** I do apologize.
A Thanks for calling. Have a nice day.	**B** You too. Goodbye.

Sample dialogue:

Student A: Can I have your phone number?

Student B: It's 8877-6256.

这个游戏名为“铃～铃～铃～”，这是一个卡片配对游戏，旨在帮助学生巩固一些用于日常电话交流的常用话语，如表明身份、确认对方身份、留口信等，学会如何用英语来打电话和接电话，达到交际目的。所有学生参与其中，完成一问一答的对话，在不断地“听”与“说”的过程中练习接打电话的交际用语，使课堂变得既有效率又不乏趣味。

学生在进行配对游戏的过程中，教师不要加以干涉，配对成功与否由小组成员商议，只有全员一致通过时，方能匹配成功。教师可以在游戏结束后再核对学生的配对是否正确，然后带领学生一起讨论卡片上出现的话语，分析每句话的功能意图，也可以稍加拓展，补充一些其他的表达方式。最后还可以让学生两人一组，模拟打电话的场景，完成一个更长更完整的对话，帮助学生进一步巩固打电话和接电话的语言表达。

 Sale or Exchange

Focus: Asking About Price, Bargaining

Level: Intermediate

Duration: 20～25 minutes

Procedure:

- Explain the rules:

  (1) Every student has $300 and 5 items at the beginning of the game. Students can buy, sell or exchange items. They must get as many items and as much money as possible to win the game.

  (2) The prices printed on the item cards are just for reference. Students can sell their items at any price and buyers can bargain to cut the cost of the items.

  (3) Students can exchange their items for others' or for others' money.

  (4) If students have the five items as requested in their instructions at the end of the game, they can get a $300 bonus.

  (5) After each deal, they must record the name of the person they trade with and the money they spend or make.

- Give each student an instruction card and five separate item cards.
- The students move around, buying, selling or exchanging items. They must keep a correct record of each deal.
- Go around, monitoring, collecting some good sentences or wrong sentences from the students and writing them down on the blackboard.
- The students total their items' value (the prices printed on their item cards), the money left and their bonus. The person with the most money wins.
- Give feedback, praising positive language use as well as correcting the errors written on the blackboard.

○ 在游戏过程中，教师尽量不介入学生的对话，而是在一旁观察学生运用询价、议价的交际用语的情况，并在黑板上记下一些学生说的好句和错句，游戏结束后再进行反馈。

Examples:

Sample of instruction cards and item cards:

Now you have $300 and five items. You must buy, sell or exchange items to make money. At the end of the game, you will get a $300 bonus if you have got **five pieces of jewellery**.				
Instruments guitar $50	**Toys** popgun $75	**Jewellery** bracelet $100	**Clothing** dress $125	**Furniture** sofa $150

Now you have $300 and five items. You must buy, sell or exchange items to make money. At the end of the game, you will get a $300 bonus if you have got **five pieces of furniture**.				
Jewellery brooch $50	**Clothing** blouse $75	**Furniture** chair $100	**Instruments** saxophone $125	**Toys** puppet $150

○ 教师可以根据学生情况或课堂话题来更改物品的种类、价格等，以保证游戏顺利进行。

Now you have $300 and five items. You must buy, sell or exchange items to make money. At the end of the game, you will get a $300 bonus if you have got **five pieces of clothing**.				
Toys toy car $50	**Jewellery** ring $75	**Clothing** jacket $100	**Furniture** wardrobe $125	**Instruments** piano $150

Now you have $300 and five items. You must buy, sell or exchange items to make money. At the end of the game, you will get a $300 bonus if you have got **five toys**.				
Furniture desk $50	**Instruments** drum $75	**Toys** doll $100	**Jewellery** necklace $125	**Clothing** suit $150

Now you have $300 and five items. You must buy, sell or exchange items to make money. At the end of the game, you will get a $300 bonus if you have got **five instruments**.				
Clothing T-shirt $50	**Furniture** table $75	**Instruments** violin $100	**Toys** teddy $125	**Jewellery** earrings $150

Sample dialogue:

Student A: Hi, Joyce. Do you have any toys?

Student B: Yes, I have a toy car.

Student A: How much is it?

Student B: It's $80.

Student A: That's too expensive. Can you do better on the price? How about $60?

Student B: $70. That's the best I can do.

Student A: OK. I'll take it.

这个游戏名为“出售或交换”，旨在帮助学生复习表示问价、议价的交际用语。在游戏中，每个人都拥有相同金额的钱和不同类别的物品，他们可以出售或与他人交换自己手中的物品。学生在真实的情境中进行对话，实现有意义的交际，而不是机械性地操练句型。该游戏还具有一定的竞争性，学生需要尽可能多地收集物品和赚钱，如果集满五个同类别的物品，还可以获得额外的奖金。这样的游戏规则能促使学生与不同的人进行对话，让更多的学生参与到课堂中，也让他们有更多的机会操练。

教师要充分给予学生进行对话的空间，鼓励多样化的表达，如果学生的话语中出现了错误，不要急于去打断、纠正学生，可以将错误记下来，在游戏结束后再进行集中评价和反馈，这样可以让学生在比较轻松的环境下进行交流，也能帮助学生进一步明确如何正确运用问价、议价的交际用语。

90 I'd Like to Make a Complaint!

Focus: Complaining, Apologizing, Making Requests

Level: Intermediate

Duration: 15~20 minutes

Procedure:

- Set the context by telling the students that they are going to make complaints and requests according to the key words and pictures on the cards.

- Hand out the cards, one for each student.
- The students read their own card and write on the back of the card whom they are going to complain to (e.g. a receptionist) and where they will be (e.g. in a hotel).
- Ask the students to hold their cards correctly so that the front side (the side with a picture and key words) is facing themselves and the back side (the side they have written on) is facing their partners.
- The students move around, choosing a partner at random. Using the cards as prompts, they complain, apologize and make requests in pairs. When they have finished, they swap their cards with each other and find a new partner to have a conversation with so that they can make different complaints, apologies and requests.
- Select pairs to perform their conversations. Let the audience evaluate their performances.

○ 最后，教师可以邀请几组同学在全班面前进行角色扮演，让其他同学评价他们的表演，并借此向学生传递信息：投诉时要有礼貌，提要求时要合理，道歉时要有诚意。

Examples:

Sample card:

Complaint: air-conditioner in hotel room not working

Request: change a room

(front side)

○ 卡片有正反两面，正面印有图片和关键词，提示学生投诉方要提出的投诉内容和要求。学生在充分理解卡片上的信息后，在卡片背面填写被投诉方的人物角色和地点。

Person: ____________________

Place: ____________________

(back side)

Sample dialogue:

Student A: Excuse me. The air-conditioner in my room doesn't work.

Student B: I'm terribly sorry, sir. I'll send someone to repair it right away.

Student A: This may take too long. I'd like to change a room, please.

Student B: OK. I'll arrange a new room for you.

Student A: Thank you.

Student B: You're welcome.

这个游戏名为“我要投诉！”，是一个角色扮演游戏，可以帮助学生在情境中运用恰当语言来提出投诉和回应投诉，实现交际目的。这个游戏的趣味在于为学生设置了各种真实的生活场景，如酒店、商店、餐馆等。学生在不同的场景下进行角色扮演，每个场景需要两名角色，如房客与酒店前台、买家与卖家、顾客与服务员。每个学生扮演的角色都不是固定的，他们需要不停切换角色，既要扮演提出投诉的一方，如房客、买家、顾客，向不同的人提出投诉，比如，向酒店前台投诉房间设备问题、向卖家投诉商品质量问题、向服务员投诉菜品问题等，并且提出相应的要求；也要扮演被投诉的一方，如酒店前台、卖家、服务员等，需要回应投诉方的投诉和要求。

这个游戏不仅可以有效地帮助学生复习巩固一些常用的交际用语，也能让学生真切地体会到在真实的人际交往中，作为提出投诉的一方，即使再生气也要选择用礼貌的方式来说明问题、表达情绪和表明态度，只有这样才有利于解决问题；而作为回应投诉的一方，要及时地致以歉意，安抚对方的情绪，弥补过失。

91 Where Can I...?

Focus: Asking and Guiding the Way

Level: Intermediate

Duration: 10～15 minutes

Procedure:

- Divide the class into pairs—A and B, and give each student a corresponding map. Student A gets an incomplete map (Map A) while student B gets a complete one (Map B) .
- Both students A and B should finish their tasks according to the instructions on their maps. Student A, as a newcomer, has to ask

○ 教师需强调：A 同学可以通过再次询问等方式来确定目的地的位置，但不可以直接看 B 同学的地图来获取信息。

the way while student B needs to help student A to find the destinations by giving directions. To double check whether student A fully understands the instructions, he/she is supposed to repeat the directions, mark the routes and write down the names of the building on his/her map.

Examples:

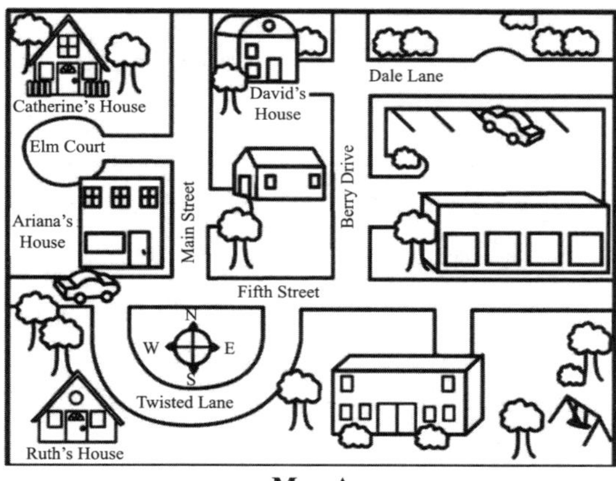

Map A

> **Instructions on Map A:**
> You are Ruth, a newcomer in Spring Town. Here are the things you want to do: buy weekly groceries, buy some flowers, borrow a book and learn English.

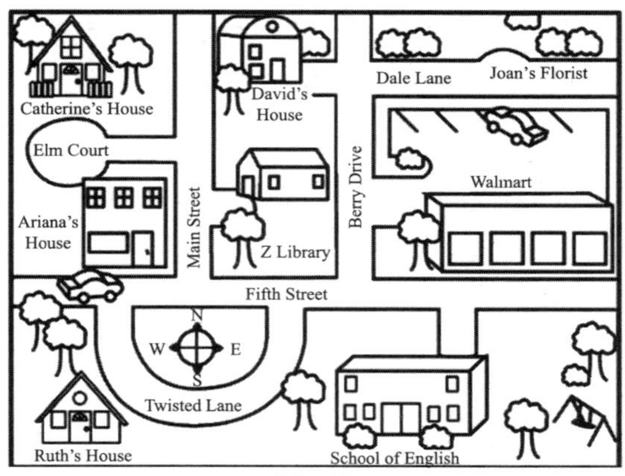

Map B

> **Instructions on Map B:**
> You are David, who has lived in Spring Town for many years. You are going to help Ruth, the newcomer to get familiar with the town.

Sample dialogue:

Student A: David, could you help me get familiar with the surroundings?

Student B: Sure.

Student A: Thanks. Now what troubles me most is my poor English. I am thinking of improving it. Could you recommend a place for me to learn English?

Student B: Well, I think you might go to School of English.

Student A: Is it near my home?

Student B: Yes. You can walk there. First, turn right and walk along Twisted Lane. Next, turn right into Fifth Street and walk along Fifth Street. You will find the path to the school on your right.

Student A: Let me check again, David. First, turn right and walk along Twisted Lane. Next, turn right into Fifth Street and walk along Fifth Street. The path to the school is on my right. Am I right?

Student B: Yes, exactly.

这个游戏叫做“我可以去哪里……？”，旨在帮助学生操练问路、指路的交际用语。该活动的挑战在于学生是否能正确给出指令，以及根据指令在地图上画出线路图并标注出地点名称。通过创设真实的交际情境，学生能够更有效地进行语言实践。游戏过后，教师可以检测学生在游戏中的参与情况。譬如：邀请几组学生上台做对话展示，并要求其他学生边听边判断语言是否正确；又或是选择某位拿到地图 A 的同学，将其完成的地图做投影展示，通过全班复述路线，对该地图上的标注进行核查。最后，教师还可以引导学生将问路和指路的核心词句进行归纳整理，并关注不同句型的语调，以此巩固所学，使交际更加自然有效。

92 Help the Simpsons!

Focus: Offering Advice and Suggestions

Level: Intermediate

Duration: 10～15 minutes

Procedure:

- Divide the whole class into several groups of 4. Each group is given a picture of the Simpsons on which is the description of the problem they meet and some key words as well.
- All the group members have a discussion and decide the characters they want to act as. Each group member should think of one or two sentences to describe the problem in detail. The key words are just for reference.

> ○ 学生首次进行游戏时，可能会比较局限于图片上的描述。教师可以在学生讨论的过程中，引导学生关注关键词，鼓励学生打开思路。

- After preparation, the groups take turns to go to the stage and act as the Simpsons. They should tell the audience the problem they meet and ask for advice or suggestions.
- The audience try to offer advice or suggestions. If the advice or suggestion is taken, the student can win one point for his/ her group.
- The group with the highest points will be given the title of *"The Sweet Big Sister/Brother"* .

> ○ 对于建议是否可以被采纳，学生一开始会比较迷茫。此时教师可以适当提醒学生，建议是否合理可行，最终决定权在学生。

Examples:

The picture and the description:

Bart is always playing computer games and he's even got some health problems. The other family members are worried about him.
headache / worried...

> ○ 教师可以找一些比较贴近学生生活的问题，比如健康、交友、电子游戏、学习方法等，让交际具有实际意义。

Sample dialogue:

Mr Simpson: My son is always playing computer games and I don't know what to do.

Student A: You'd better have a talk with him.

Mr Simpson: I'll take your advice.

这个游戏名为“帮助辛普森一家”，以辛普森一家所遇到的问题为背景，创造符合日常生活的情境，让学生在此情境下进行交际，提出建议。之所以选择“辛普森一家”为载体，不仅是因为他们比较著名，更是因为其中的角色性格迥异，主角年龄和初中生相仿，他们身上所发生的故事、他们会遇到的问题比较能引起学生的共鸣。当然，教师也可以利用其他丰富的影视、漫画资源。

在人际交往中，“提出建议”是重要的学习内容，要求学生在书面或者口头交际中，恰当运用语言来表达并回应，达到交际目的。这个游戏主要分为两部分，第一部分是各小组根据自己所拿到的“辛普森一家”的问题描述，头脑风暴他们可能会遇到的具体困难，并组织语言正确表达出来；第二部分则是其他小组成员根据台上小组所描述的问题，运用常见的句型，给出建议。

这个游戏的得分与否不是由教师决定，而是由台上的“辛普森一家”来决定。也就是说，只有当这个建议符合当时的情境，合情合理时，才可以被采纳，才能拿到相应的分数。这在一定程度上也是向学生传递这样的信息：我们需要根据不同的情况，提出适切的建议，让交际更加有效。

93 Super Polite

Focus: Making Inquiries Politely

Level: Intermediate

Duration: 20～25 minutes

Procedure:

- Help the students learn how to make inquiries politely and write some expressions on the board.
- Divide the students into pairs (Student A and B). Give each student a corresponding role card. Tell them to read their role card.
- In pairs, the students do the first role-play. Student A plays the role of a ticket agent, while Student B plays the role of a customer, asking for information about a flight. Afterwards, the pairs swap their roles and move on to the second role-play.
- When the students have finished, ask some pairs to act out their dialogue in front of the class and give feedback.

Examples:

Sample expression list:

Expression list
Excuse me, ... Pardon me, ... I'd like to know... I wonder... Do you know... Could you tell me...

○ 教师要提醒学生，可在直接问句前加 Excuse me 或 Pardon me 表示礼貌，此时，原问句语序不发生变化。若将直接问句改为间接问句询问信息时，要注意原问句语序的变化。

Sample role cards:

Student A

At the ticket office: ticket agent

You work at a ticket office for American Airways. Answer Student B' s questions using the following information.

A flight from New York to Washington			
Departure time	10:00	Arrival time	11:15
Class	Business	Economy	
Price	$199	$75	
Baggage weight restriction	23kgs	5kgs	
Meal	One meal included	No meal	

○ 该游戏设定了机场售票处这一场景以及售票代理人和顾客两个角色，要求学生角色扮演。教师也可以加入更多的场景设定，比如酒店前台、火车站售票处、电影院售票处等，再根据不同的场景设定多样的角色。

At the ticket office: customer

You want to book a flight from New York to Chicago. Politely ask Student B for information about the flight and complete the missing information in the table.

A flight from New York to Chicago			
Departure time		Arrival time	
Class	Business	Economy	
Price			
Baggage weight restriction			
Meal			

When you have all the information, decide if you want to fly business or economy.

Student B

At the ticket office: customer

You want to book a flight from New York to Washington. Politely ask Student A for information about the flight and complete the missing information in the table.

A flight from New York to Washington				
Departure time		Arrival time		
Class	Business		Economy	
Price				
Baggage weight restriction				
Meal				

When you have all the information, decide if you want to fly business or economy.

At the ticket office: ticket agent

You work at a ticket office for American Airways. Answer Student A's questions using the following information.

A flight from New York to Chicago				
Departure time	13:30	Arrival time		16:10
Class	Business		Economy	
Price	$228		$106	
Baggage weight restriction	30kgs		10kgs	
Meal	One meal included		One meal included	

Sample dialogue:

Student A: Hello, can I help you?

Student B: Yes, I'd like know if there's any flight from New York to Washington today.

Student A: We only have one flight today.

Student B: Could you tell me when it will depart?

Student A: It will depart at 10 o'clock in the morning.

Student B: Do you know how long it will take?

Student A: It will take one hour and fifteen minutes.

Student B: I wonder how much the ticket is?

Student A: A business class ticket is $199 and an economy class ticket is $75.

Student B: May I ask what the baggage weight restriction is?

Student A: The baggage restriction is 23kgs for business class and 5kgs for economy.

Student B: I also wonder whether meals will be served on the flight?

Student A: There is no meal for economy class passengers and one meal is served for business class passengers.

Student B: OK. I'll take one economy class ticket.

这个游戏名为“超级礼貌”，这是一个角色扮演游戏，旨在帮助学生练习运用恰当的语言来礼貌地询问信息，达到交际目的。在日常生活中，学生可以用直接问句来询问信息，但如果面对的是一个陌生人，这样就会显得不太礼貌。因此，这个游戏将重点放在学生如何更有礼貌地询问信息。游戏开始前，教师需提前教授一些礼貌地询问信息的表达方式，比如，可在直接问句前加 Excuse me/ Pardon me，或者将直接问句改为间接问句，后者较前者要显得更礼貌、更正式。该游戏鼓励学生尽可能多地用间接问句来进行提问，巩固礼貌询问信息的语言表达。

94 Doctor! Doctor!

Focus: Describing Illnesses and Symptoms, Asking for and Giving Advice

Level: Intermediate

Duration: 20～25 minutes

Procedure:

- Turn the classroom into a surgery. Arrange a waiting where all the patients sit, and several consulting rooms where the doctors talk to and examine the patients. The following picture shows the classroom arrangement.

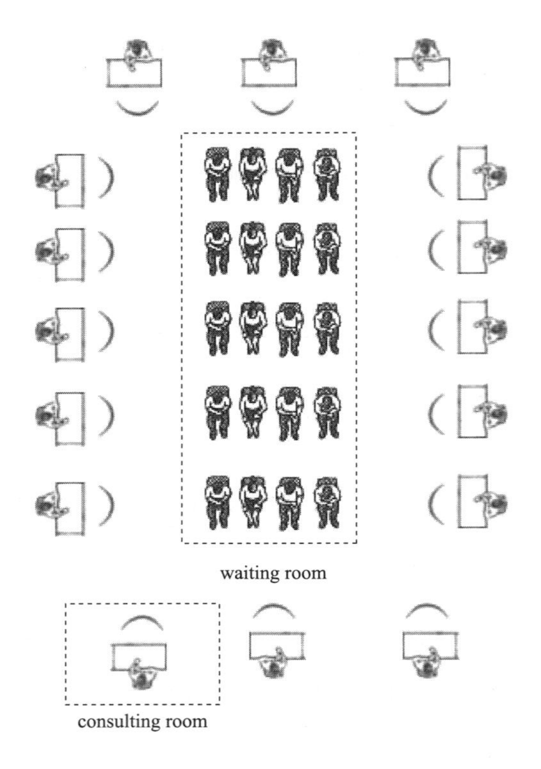

- Divide the students into two groups: the patient group and the doctor group. Hand out the illness tables to the students. Ask the patient group to brainstorm what the causes and symptoms are and ask the doctor group to brainstorm what medical advice they will give. Then give out the patient cards to the patient group, and the doctor cards to the doctor group. Give them two minutes to read through their card and prepare what they are going to say.

○ 教师根据学生数量进行分组，确保患者组的人数多于医生组的人数即可。

- The students do the role-play. The patients sit in the waiting room until the doctors call them into their consulting rooms. Every patient chooses one illness from the illness table and visits three different doctors, describing his/her symptoms and asking for advice. After each visit, the patients return to the waiting room. Every doctor can receive any number of patients, but can only see one patient at a time. The doctors ask the patients questions and examine them, then make proper diagnoses and give some medical advice.

- When the students have finished, ask the patients to choose the best doctor and give reasons.

Examples:

Sample of the illness table:

Illness	Cause	Symptom	Advice
a cold			
the flu			
a headache			
a stomachache			
a toothache			
a cut			
a broken arm/leg			

○ 表中列举了几种常见疾病，教师可以根据教学情况做增减。该表格用于学生分组进行头脑风暴环节，病人组讨论病因和症状，医生组讨论治疗方案，为之后的角色扮演做铺垫。

Sample of the patient card and doctor card:

Patient Card

You are a patient. Choose one illness from the illness table and visit three doctors to see who gives the best treatment for your illness. You should tell the doctors:

- what your symptoms are.
- how long you have had the symptoms.
- what caused your illness.

Doctor Card

You are a doctor. When you are free, call one patient into your consulting room. You should:

- ask questions and examine the patient.
- tell what you think the patient's illness is.
- give some medical advice.

Sample dialogue:

Student A: Good morning, doctor.

Student B: Good morning. How can I help you?

Student A: I'm feeling unwell and having a slight fever and a sore throat.

Student B: How long have you had these symptoms?

Student A: About two days ago. But it's getting worse.

Student B: Do you have any other symptoms?

Student A: I have a runny nose and can't stop sneezing. Also, I have a bad cough.

Student B: Let me examine you. Open your mouth wide and say Ah!

Student A: Ah!

Student B: Let me listen to your lungs. Take deep breaths.

Student A: Hoo, hoo, hoo!

Student B: It sounds like you've got the flu. I'm writing you the prescription and you can buy the medicine from the pharmacy.

Student A: OK. How should I take the medicine?

Student B: Take one pill a day.

Student A: Should I take the pills after meal or before meal?

Student B: After meal.

Student A: What else should I do?

Student B: You should have light food and drink lots of water. Also, you should get plenty of rest.

Student A: OK. Thank you, doctor.

这个游戏名为“医生！医生！”，这是一个角色扮演游戏，旨在帮助学生练习运用恰当的语言来描述病症、寻求建议和提供建议，达到交际目的。在游戏开始前，教师需要改变教室布局，重新摆放桌椅，模拟真实的就医场景，设立一个等候室和若干诊疗室，各个诊疗室与等候室之间应隔开一定的距离。如此，可以使学生在扮演角色时更有代入感，并且还能培养学生有序就医的意识。比如，患者必须在医生的允许下方能进入诊疗室；当诊疗室已经有一位患者时，其他患者只能在等候室等待，给医生和患者留有一对一谈话的私密空间，以保护患者的隐私。在角色扮演之前，鼓励学生先以小组形式进行头脑风暴，讨论如何描述病症和寻求建议，以及提供何种治疗方案，为之后学生进行角色扮演搭建语言支架，降低游戏难度。

95 Do You Agree?

Focus: Giving Opinions, Agreeing and Disagreeing

Level: Advanced

Duration: 20～25 minutes

Procedure:

- Divide the students into groups of 4. Give each group a set of discussion cards and four opinion cards. Ask them to put the two piles of cards face down in the middle on the table.
- The students pick a discussion card and turn it over so that everyone in the group can see it. They then shuffle the opinion cards and hand one to each student. They have 30 seconds to prepare and 2 minutes to discuss the topic on the discussion card. They must express the opinion shown on the opinion card even if they don't agree with it. When the discussion has been finis discussion card, gather up the opinion cards, shuffle them and hand them out again. After that, they conduct another discussion. The game continues until all the topics have been discussed.

○ 每个学生都要参与每一个话题的讨论，而发言的顺序和发言时间都不作要求，由学生自行决定，但要鼓励学生尽可能多地表达自己的想法。

○ 卡片有两类，分别是讨论卡和观点卡。讨论卡上的内容是学生在游戏中需要讨论的话题。教师可以选择一些热点话题或是贴近学生生活实际的话题。观点卡上的内容则决定了学生在话题讨论时所持的立场。

Examples:

Sample of discussion cards:

Pop singers and film stars get paid too much.	The most important thing about a job is the salary.
All genetically-modified food should be banned.	Hollywood films are much better than local films.
Teenagers shouldn't be allowed to play computer games.	Good English learners must have the perfect American or British accent.

Sample of opinion cards:

You agree.	You disagree.
You don't have a strong opinion.	You are free to give your own opinion.

Sample dialogue:

Student A: In my opinion, teenagers shouldn't be allowed to play computer games. The reason is that playing computer games is a waste of time. It can cause a decline in academic performance.

Students B: I totally agree with you. Nowadays, a large number of teenagers are addicted to computer games, which has a negative influence on their health and study.

Student C: I really can't agree with you there. Much of the negative effects of playing computer games results from excessive amounts of use. But that doesn't mean playing computer games is bad. Actually, there are many developmental games which benefit teenagers. I think teenagers should be allowed to play computer games.

Student D: I agree. Teenagers can play computer games, but there must be a limitation.

这个游戏名为“你同意吗？”，这是一个卡片游戏，旨在帮助学生巩固表示赞同与不赞同的句型，使学生能够运用恰当的语言来表达个人观点，达到交际目的。在游戏中，四人为一组，学生围绕一个个话题展开讨论，每个人都要表达对这些话题的看法，但学生在表达观点时是有一定限制的，他们必须按照所持观点卡上的要求来阐述观点，即使这个要求与他们心里所想是背道而驰的。而在每次开展新一轮的讨论时，学生都要重新洗牌，再次抽选一张观点卡，并且继续根据所持观点卡上的要求来展开话题讨论。这样特别的游戏设定有两方面的原因，一方面是让每个学生都有机会操练到表示赞同与不赞同的句型；另一方面是锻炼学生的批判性思维能力，使学生改变惯性思维，注意到事物的多面性，学会从多角度考虑问题。

96 Have It Rescheduled!

Focus: Changing an Appointment on the Phone

Level: Advanced

Duration: 15~20 minutes

Procedure:

- Ask students to read the email and check Jenny's plan on September 21 to find out what problem she faces.
- Guide students to go over the process of changing an appointment by completing the conversation flow.
- Divide students into pairs (A and B). Student A gets Jenny's weekly schedule while student B is provided with Doctor Martin's. Each pair needs to help Jenny reschedule her appointment with Doctor Martin. By avoiding looking at the other's seven-day agenda directly, students are required to exchange information orally by making a phone call.

○ 游戏中，学生需通过对话交换信息。为避免学生直接看到对方手上的日程表，教师可以事先调整学生的座位，让每一组的AB两位同学面对面坐着进行对话。

Examples:

<table>
<tr><td colspan="2">Jenny has just received an email from Tim. Please read it carefully and check her plan on September 21 and find out what problem she faces.</td></tr>
<tr><td>The email</td><td>Meeting on Marketing Strategy
收件人：Jenny@shet.edu.cn
抄送/密送：
主题：Meeting on Marketing Strategy
Hi Jenny,
I am sorry to tell you that we will have an emergency meeting tomorrow, September 21 at 4 pm. We will mainly talk about the current problems and go over the marketing strategy. The meeting will be held in meeting room C (1st floor). It is likely that we won't be able to get off work on time. Sorry for the inconvenience.
All the best,
Tim</td></tr>
<tr><td>Jenny's plan for September 21</td><td><table><tr><td></td><td>September 21 Tuesday</td></tr><tr><td>9 am</td><td>Stand-up meeting</td></tr><tr><td>11 am</td><td>Customer introduction</td></tr><tr><td>2 pm</td><td>Prepare demo</td></tr><tr><td>4 pm</td><td>Go to see the dentist</td></tr></table></td></tr>
<tr><td>Questions</td><td>1. What problem does Jenny have?
2. What does she need to do?</td></tr>
</table>

Work in pairs and complete the conversation flow by arranging the situations along with the language.	
Situation	Language used
A. Explaining the problem	H. —Hello, this is... How may I help you? —Hello, this is...
B. Checking the last appointment	I. —I am afraid I can't... —That's all right.
C. Confirming the new appointment	J. —What day was your appointment on? —It was on... —What time was it scheduled for? —It was for...
D. Rejecting a suggestion	K —Hold on, please. (A few seconds later) I am afraid I am not available that day/during that period.
E. Suggesting again and agreeing to a time	L. —Well, what about...? —Let me check my calendar again. (A few seconds later) Yes, that works for me.
F. Greeting and introducing yourself	M. —Oh, yes, I see your appointment. So what day would you like to switch to? —How about...? Is that OK for you?
G. Suggesting another time	N. —Oh, that would be great. —So I will put you down for (the time)... —Thank you so much. —You're welcome. See you then. Goodbye. —Goodbye.

○ 此环节需要学生理清对话顺序，再配对相应的语言表达。如果教师认为这两项任务合在一起难度较高，可以有选择性地将一侧的顺序事先固定下来。同样地，如果学生程度较好，可以将左侧 situation 一栏的部分动词进行挖空处理；或者以全班头脑风暴的方式讨论某些句型的表达。

Conversation flow	
Situation	Language used

Jenny's weekly schedule

WEEKLY SCHEDULE

	September 20 Monday	September 21 Tuesday	September 22 Wednesday	September 23 Thursday	September 24 Friday	September 25 Saturday	September 26 Sunday
9 am		Stand-up meeting	Sales team meeting on Dingding	Stand-up meeting	on a business trip to Hangzhou		
11 am		Customer introduction		Check the roadmap			
2 pm		Prepare demo	Customer demo				
4 pm		Go to see the dentist	Discuss the contract	Presentation			

Doctor Martin's weekly schedule

WEEKLY SCHEDULE

	September 20 Monday	September 21 Tuesday	September 22 Wednesday	September 23 Thursday	September 24 Friday	September 25 Saturday	September 26 Sunday
9 am							
11 am							
2 pm							
4 pm							

booked available

这个游戏叫做“改期”，旨在帮助学生在理解巩固句型的基础上，进行实战对话演练。日常生活中，经常会碰到需要更改预约的情形，因此了解更改预约的句型表达并通过真实情境进行对话操练是非常有必要的。

游戏中，学生需要通过阅读邮件以及核对 Jenny 的日程表来判断出她无法如约看牙医的情境设定。在该游戏中，学生需要自己去发现问题，进而思考电话更改预约的基本步骤以及所需要使用的语言；然后根据双方拿到的一周日程安排表，以对话的方式交换信息，确定时间后进行重新预约。最后的游戏环节，也考察了学生从文本素材中获取信息及转换信息的能力，因此这是一个以读为输入、以说为输出，以输入为基础、以输出为驱动的具有挑战难度的游戏。

97 Moral Dilemmas

Focus: Explanation and Persuasion

Level: Advanced

Duration: 30 minutes

Procedure:

- Write *Moral Dilemma* on the board and ask what it means. If no one knows it, explain and give an example:

  Your friend likes to take part in a singing contest. He sings a song to you and asks what you think. It sounds really awful. If you tell him the truth, he will be hurt. But if you say you like it, you will be lying, and people might laugh at him when he sings it in the competition.

- Ask the class what they would do in this example and why. Ask the class to brainstorm moral dilemmas they have been in.

○ 让学生举例是为了确认学生已理解 Moral Dilemmas 的涵义，以确保后续活动顺利开展。

- Give out cards to each pair. (They cannot look at each other’s cards.) Ask them to imagine this is a real situation. They should think how they would feel in the situation and make a

○ 教师可自行设计 Moral Dilemmas 的例子供学生使用，数量建议在 4 个左右。

conversation. Tell them to try to agree on an answer to the problems in the situation.

Examples:

A

- Your best friend who had been studying abroad contacted you recently. You two are going on a trip together next weekend for your 14th birthday.
- You have been acting strangely for a couple of days. You want to tell your parents your plan.
- You are worried. You think there is something that they are not telling you. Maybe they have got some problems.
- You really want to travel with your old friend. That stops you thinking about your parents.
- TELL YOUR PARENTS YOUR PL AN!

B

- You are arranging a surprise party for your kid's 14th birthday next weekend.
- You happened to hear your kid talking about his/her travel plan.
- You can't tell your kid about the party. That would make the people who have worked hard to arrange the party disappointed.
- Maybe your kid would prefer to travel, but if you tell him/her about the party, he/she will feel bad and come even if he/she does not want to.
- YOUR KID IS GOING TO TELL YOU SOME NEWS!

- Ask if anyone found an answer. Invite the good pairs to repeat their best performances for the class.

该游戏名为“道德困境”，通过设定生活中一些进退维谷的真实情境，让学生置身其中进行英语对话，从而练习使用恰当的语言对他人进行解释、劝说等。

日常生活中，使用解释、劝说等语言有诸多实际意义，例如，可以帮助销售产品或服务，可以说服人们接受观点或想法。而本活动就是为了帮助学生训练该技能。

需要注意的是，教师在活动开始前要帮助学生理解道德困境的概念，以保障后续操练可以顺利进行。此外，由于该活动对学生口语能力有较高的要求，因此，活动过程中，教师要时时巡视、随时提供帮助。

98 Nice to Meet You

Focus: Asking for and Giving Personal Information

Level: All levels

Duration: 15~20 minutes

Procedure:

- Help the students to brainstorm the questions which they might ask a person they want to know.
- Divide the students into two groups. Make an inner circle of the students facing outwards and an outer circle of the students facing inwards.
- The students form a pair with the one opposite, asking for and giving personal information. After about two minutes, the outer circle moves one step to the right, thus creating new pairs, repeating what they did in the last round. The game continues until the outer circle moves back to the original place.
- Invite several students to introduce their classmates to the class, using the information they found out.

> ○ 在游戏过程中，学生互相询问个人信息，可以用之前头脑风暴时列出的问题进行提问，也可以是在对话过程中延伸的问题。

Examples:

Sample dialogue:

Student A: Hi, I'm Josh. May I have your name?

Student B: Hi, Josh. My name is Amy. Nice to meet you.

Student A: Nice to meet you too. Where are you from?

Student B: I'm from Shanghai. How about you?

Student A: I'm from Beijing. Have you ever been to Beijing?

Student B: No, I haven't been there before. Have you got any pets?

Student A: Yes, I have a dog and a cat.

Student B: Really! I also have a dog.

这个游戏名为“很高兴遇见你”，这是一个破冰游戏，旨在帮助学生练习运用恰当的语言来询问及说明个人信息，如姓名、生日、爱好等，达到交际目的。游戏开始前，教师可以帮助学生进行头脑风暴，讨论对于初次见面的人可以问些什么问题，为学生之后进行游戏作好铺垫。游戏过程中，学生围成一个内圈和一个外圈，内圈与外圈同学一对一、面对面站立，两两之间进行两分钟的对话，询问对方的个人信息。每两分钟后，外圈同学向右移动一步，然后与内圈同学组成新的两人一组进行对话。最后，教师可以邀请几位同学利用对话时收集到的信息向全班介绍一位他们刚认识的同学。

这个游戏非常适合新生的第一课，学生彼此之间并不熟悉，而这个游戏既能帮助学生快速地认识彼此，又能帮助学生巩固用于询问个人信息的语言。这个游戏可操作性强且适用性广，它不需要任何道具，随时随地就可以进行，它也可以运用于任何年龄段、任何水平的学生。

此外，教师还可以借由这个游戏帮助学生意识到文化差异性，英语文化非常注重隐私。因此，在日常交流中，面对初次见面的人，要谨慎地选择聊天的话题，不宜问一些涉及隐私的、敏感性强的问题，如对方年龄、体重、宗教信仰等，可以从兴趣爱好、学习经历等方面展开询问，寻找共同话题，避免尴尬的情况出现。

99 Lost and Found

Focus: Describing Things

Level: All levels

Duration: 10～15 minutes

Procedure:

- Set the context by telling the students that they lost something yesterday and they are going to find their lost items.
- Divide the students into two groups. Give out the lost cards to one group, and the found cards to the other group. Make sure that every student has at least three cards.
- The students who have the lost cards move around, describing their lost items

to the students who have the found cards. The students with the found cards remain in their seats, waiting to be asked. They can ask more questions to identify the person who lost the item and then give the lost item to the owner. The game continues until all the students who have the lost cards find their lost items.

○ 在游戏过程中，一半学生扮演失主，另一半则扮演失物招领处的职员。若失主在描述物品时过于模糊，那么职员可以进一步询问物品的细节特征，以确认对方丢失的物品究竟是哪一个。

- The students swap their roles and play the game.
- Select pairs to make a dialogue in front of the class.

Examples:

Sample of lost cards:

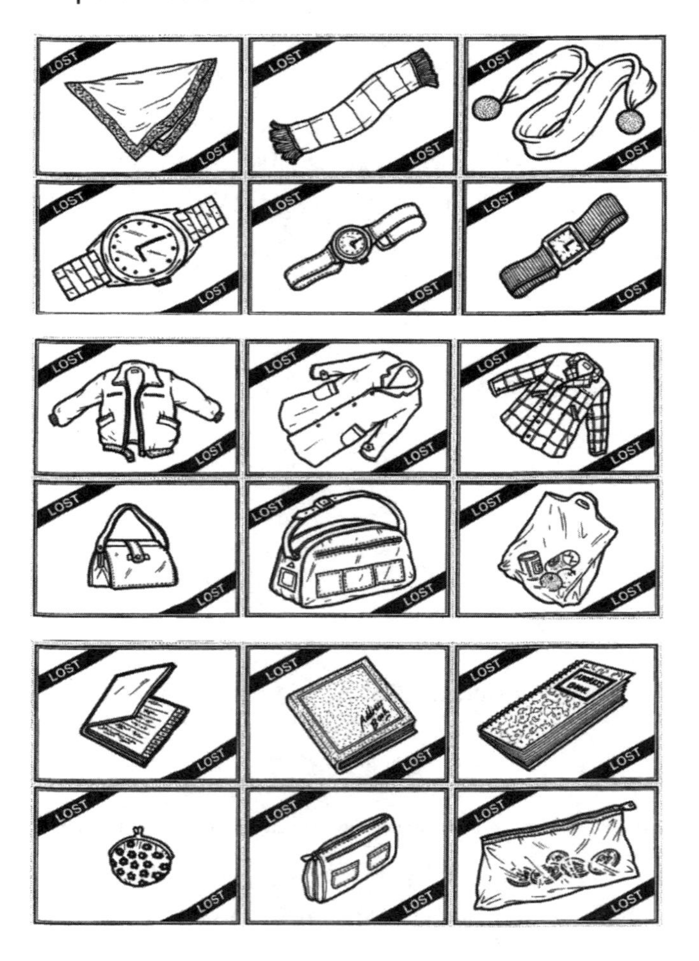

○ 卡片上的图片是学生在游戏中需要进行描述的物品，教师在选择物品时，同一类别里至少要有三个具有不同特征的物品。以围巾类为例，选择至少三条不同的围巾，可以是不同材质、颜色或图案的，以便学生能更具体地谈论物品的特征。

Sample of found cards:

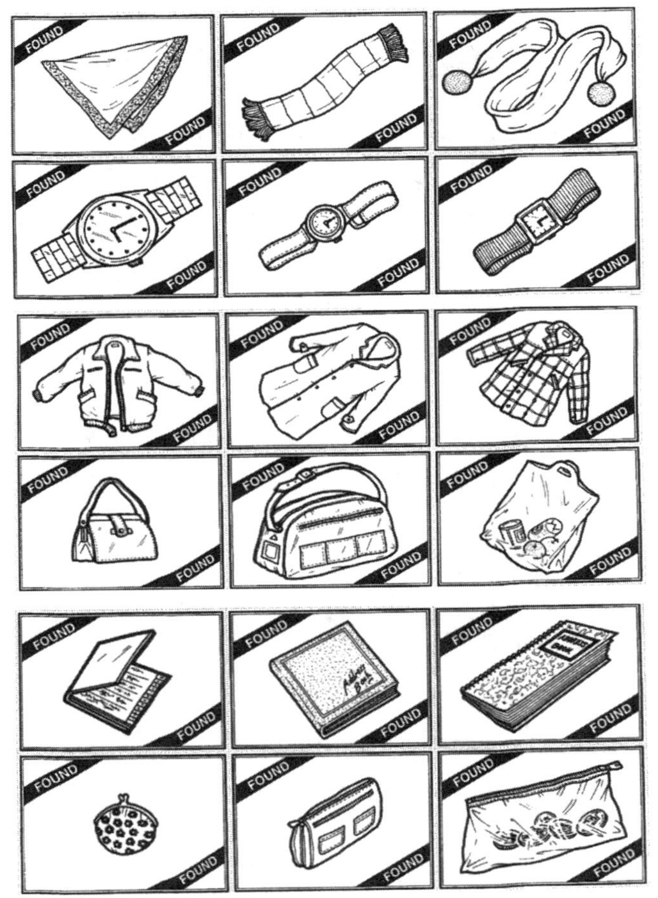

（图片来源：Kay S. Reward Elementary: Resource Pack [M] Macmillan Education, 1998.）

Sample dialogue:

Student A: Hello, may I help you?

Student B: I lost my watch yesterday. I hope I can find it here.

Student A: What does it look like?

Student B: It's a round watch.

Student A: We have several round watches here. Can you describe your watch in more detail?

Student B: The strap is made of leather.

Student A: OK. Let me take a look. Is this your watch?

Student B: Yes, it's mine. Thanks!

Student A: You're welcome. Bye.

这个游戏名为“失物招领”，这是一个角色扮演游戏，旨在帮助学生练习运用恰当的语言来询问及描述物品的特征，如尺寸、形状、材质等，达到交际目的。这个游戏真实地模拟了学生生活中常见的失物招领的场景，学生扮演失主和失物招领处的职员进行对话，一方描述，一方询问，学生在一来一回的对话过程中自然而然地巩固了用于描述物品特征的语言，完成交际任务。而且，由于角色需要，学生还能同时操练一些用于表达问候、感激的交际用语。

这个游戏适用于各种水平的学生，教师可以按需调整物品的种类和数量，以此来提高或降低游戏的难度，满足不同层次学生的需求。

100 Restaurant Role-Play

Focus: Conversational Language for Ordering

Level: All levels

Duration: 20~25 minutes

Procedure:

- Divide the class into two groups (15 students for each). Each group will name their own restaurant.
- In each restaurant, decide 3 cooks, 3 waiters, 3 groups of customers. One waiter serves one table of customers.
- Each restaurant needs to create a menu, 3 scripts about the conversation among waiters and customers. (See the sample menu and dialogue)
- The script and menu are designed for the other group to play. When creating the script, students may dramatize the plot to make it fun to act. They may create a “demanding

○ 该游戏的乐趣在于为对方组员编写剧本，学生可以发挥想象，力图让人物、对话、剧情变得生动有趣。

customer" , an "ill-mannered waiter" or a "worst cook" .

- Swap the menu and dialogue with the other restaurant to do the role-play. Give 3 minutes to prepare the play.
- During the play, cooks need to quickly draw the food and cut it. Use line image to save time.

○ 厨师组拿到订单后，用简笔画快速画出食物，递给服务员。提示厨师，他们需要观察服务员和顾客的互动情况，最后给予综合评价。教师需为学生准备纸张和画笔。

- After the play, customers, waiters and cooks need to fill in a feedback form to make comments on this experience. (See the sample form)

顾客问卷

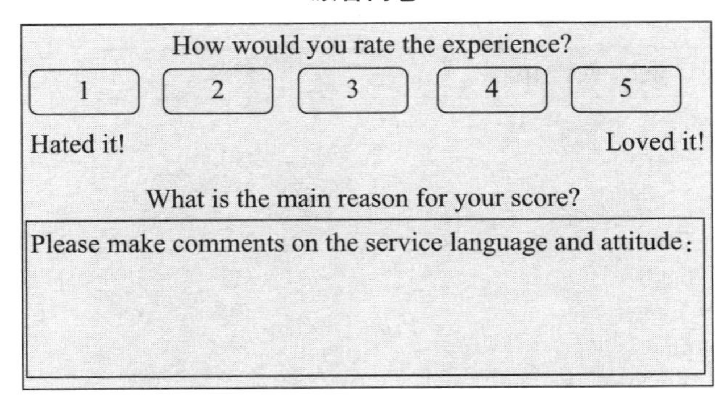

How would you rate the experience?

1	2	3	4	5

Hated it! Loved it!

What is the main reason for your score?

Please make comments on the service language and attitude:

○ 顾客需对服务员的礼貌用语做出评价。

服务员问卷

How would you rate the experience?

1	2	3	4	5

Hated it! Loved it!

What is the main reason for your score?

Please make comments on customers' language and attitude:

○ 服务员需对顾客的礼貌用语做出评价。

厨师问卷

How would you rate the experience?

1	2	3	4	5

Hated it! Loved it!

What is the main reason for your score?

Please make comments on your working experience at this restaurant.

○ 厨师可对服务员、顾客的表现做出综合评价。

Sample Menu

Bob's Restaurant	RMB
Starters	
Beef Soup	30
Garden Salad	25
Main Course	
Tuna Sandwich	35
Cheeseburger	30
Dumpling	30
Pork Ramen	35
Fried Rice	25
Sushi	25
Drinks	
Cappuccino	20
Orange Juice	15
Jasmine Tea	20

Sample dialogue:

Waiter: Welcome to Bob's Restaurant, how can I help?

C1: Yes, I'd like to have a cheeseburger.

C2: May I have some dumplings?

Waiter: Sure, Would you like a starter?

C3: Yes, I'd like a beef soup and a grilled cheese sandwich, please.

Waiter: Would you like anything to drink?

C1: Yes, I'd like a glass of Coke, please.

Waiter: Would Pepsi be OK? We don't have Coke.

C1: That would be fine.

Waiter: What about you two?

C2: We are fine with water. Can you bring us some iced water?

Waiter: Sure. I will be right back.

Waiter: (Bring the food and drink) Can I bring you anything else?

C2: No，thank you. Just the bill.

(After Lunch)

C3: Check，please.

Waiter: Certainly. That's 120 yuan in total.

C1: There you go. Thank you very much.

Waiter: You're welcome. Have a good day.

C2: You too.

此游戏叫做“餐厅角色扮演”，旨在帮助学生学会如何点菜。游戏中，学生可以发挥想象制作菜单及剧本，同时还需考虑到如何运用提供帮助、请求以及应答的交际用语（阴影部分为语言重点）。同时，教师也可参与其中，和学生共同出演可以增加趣味性。在最后的反馈表中，每个学生都能给予彼此评价。教师可根据班级的人数、语言程度来调整角色需求。

Bibliography（参考文献）

[1] 罗敏 . 英语语音教程 [M]. 北京：外语教学与研究出版社，2018.

[2] 王桂珍 . 英语语音教程（第二版）[M]. 北京：高等教育出版社，2010.

[3] 上海市教育委员会教学研究室 . 上海市初中英语学科教学基本要求 [M]. 上海：上海教育出版社，2017.

[4] [英] 安・贝克（Ann Baker）. 剑桥国际英语语音教程：英音版（修订版）[M]. 北京：北京语言大学出版社，2017.

[5] 张卓宏 . 突破英语听说要塞——连读与音变 [M]. 北京：清华大学出版社，2006.

[6] 中华人民共和国教育部 . 普通高中英语课程标准 [M]. 北京：人民教育出版社，2003.

[7] Anderson J. *Role Plays for Today: Photocopiable Activities to Get Students Speaking* [M]. Knoxville: Delta Publishing Company, 2006.

[8] Botel, M., & Paparo, L. B. *The Plainer Truths of Teaching, Learning and Literacy: A comprehensive guide to reading, writing, speaking and listening Pre-K-12 across the curriculum* [M]. Owl Publishing, LLC, 2016.

[9] Gammidge M. *Speaking Extra Book and Audio CD Pack: A Resource Book of Multi-level Skills Activities* [M]. Cambridge: Cambridge University Press, 2004.

[10] Kay S. *Reward Elementary: Resource Pack* [M]. London: Macmillan Education, 1998.

[11] Kay S. *Reward Intermediate: Resource Pack* [M]. London: Macmillan Education, 1999.

[12] Mortimer Colin. *Elements of Pronunciation* [M]. Cambridge: Cambridge University Press, 1985.

[13] Peter Watcyn-Jones. *Fun Class Activities Book 1* [M]. Edinburgh: Pearson Education Limited, 2000.

[14] Peter Watcyn-Jones. *Fun Class Activities Book 2* [M]. Edinburgh: Pearson Education Limited, 2000.

[15] Sandy Turley. *Phonics games & learning activities* [M]. Westminster: Teacher Created Resources, Inc., 1999.

[16] Suzanne W. Woodward. *Fun with Grammar* [M]. London: Prentice-Hall International Limited, 1996.

[17] 王蔷 . 连接拼读、阅读与写作教学——均衡的英语读写素养发展模式探析 [J]. 英语学习，2021(6).

图书在版编目（CIP）数据

玩游戏，学英语：英语课堂游戏活动100例／王瑛主编．—上海：华东师范大学出版社，2022
ISBN 978-7-5760-3175-1

Ⅰ.①玩…　Ⅱ.①王…　Ⅲ.①英语课—课堂教学—教案（教育）—中小学　Ⅳ.①G633.412

中国版本图书馆CIP数据核字（2022）第154179号

大夏书系·英语教学
玩游戏，学英语：英语课堂游戏活动100例

主　　编　王　瑛
责任编辑　任红瑚
责任校对　杨　坤
封面设计　淡晓库

出版发行　华东师范大学出版社
社　　址　上海市中山北路3663号　　邮编　200062
网　　址　www.ecnupress.com.cn
电　　话　021-60821666　行政传真　021-62572105
客服电话　021-62865537
邮购电话　021-62869887　地址　上海市中山北路3663号华东师范大学校内先锋路口
网　　店　http：//hdsdcbs.tmall.com/

印 刷 者　北京密兴印刷有限公司
开　　本　700×1000　16开
插　　页　1
印　　张　14
字　　数　160千字
版　　次　2022年9月第一版
印　　次　2022年9月第一次
印　　数　6 000
书　　号　ISBN 978-7-5760-3175-1
定　　价　55.00元

出 版 人　王　焰